THE COMPLETE THAI COOKBOOK

*140 Easy Recipes For Cooking At Home
Tasty Asian Food*

Maki Blanc

D1307911

THAI
COOKBOOK

70 Easy Recipes for Traditional Food from Thailand

Maki Blanc

Contents

CHAPTER 6: THE WORLD OF TRADITIONAL THAI RECIPES EATEN ONLY BY THAI PEOPLE 109

CHAPTER 3: THE WORLD OF VEGETARIAN THAI DINNER RECIPES

CHAPTER 4: THE WORLD OF VEGETARIAN THAI DESSERT

Introduction

Food is an indispensable part of our every day schedule. Without the addition of solid, nutritious, and scrumptious food, life can truly transform into a test. Cooking is viewed as a difficult task because of the lack of our cooking abilities or exposure to the authentic recipes of different cuisines.

This book is principally about Thai cuisine. Thai food is the public cooking of Thailand. Thai cooking places accentuation on light meals with amazing aromatic segments and a spicy or zesty edge. Thai cooking is about the shuffling of different components to make an amicable completion i.e. like an unpredictable melodic harmony, it must have a smooth surface, yet it does not make a difference what goes on underneath.

In this cookbook, you will come across the history and origin of Thai food as well as the history of traditional Thai dishes. You are going to get a brief information regarding the evolution of Thai cuisine over the years.

There are various health benefits of having Thai food at home, and you will know all of these benefits when you go through the different properties of spices used in Thai foods. You will get over 70 different breakfast, lunch, dinner, and dessert, and authentic recipes that are only eaten by Thai people. You can easily start cooking at home with the detailed instructions present below each recipe.

Preparing your Thai food at home without the need to order food from some restaurant can become very easy, once you start reading this book. So, why wait for more? Let us dive deep into the world of Thai cuisine.

Chapter 1: Introduction to Thai Food

Thailand is the most hailed country in the whole world for its cuisine. From the southern landmass toward the northern locales, the country offers a diverse blend of an irresistibly delightful food.

The south of Thailand is acclaimed for its blazing curries, profound usage of coconut milk, and astonishing fish plans. The northeastern part is striking for its veggie filled plates of blended greens and flavors, grilled meat, sausages, and tenacious rice. Bangkok, the greatest city, attracts Thais from all over the country to make an endless mix of alluring flavors to taste.

From streak cooked sautés to hand beaten servings of blended greens, you can find the variety of mouthwatering flavors. If you value eating, you will be in a paradise with the combination and variety of food in this cuisine.

1.1 History and Origin of Thai Food

Thai food started with the people who emigrated from the southern Chinese regions many years back to the land of Thailand. There was a great Szechwan impact on Thai cooking. In any case, all through the long haul, various things have affected Thai food.

Previously, Buddhist clerics carried an Indian touch to the food, and southern Muslim states influenced the cooking in the south of Thailand. Much later, Thai food was affected by European cooking after contact with Portuguese clergymen and Dutch merchants. During this Time, there was some effect from the Japanese as well.

Thailand is a significant country with a distinct geography, and all through the long haul, this has provoked the improvement of nearby divergences in its style of food varieties.

1.2 History of Traditional Thai Dishes

In the beginning, Thai food was usually eaten while sitting on mats or covers on the floor. These traditions are still found in the more customary and traditional families. Right now, there are four distinct styles of cooking in Traditional Thai food:

- The focal region of Thailand offers food that is somewhere between the north and south. In any case, fragrant Jasmine rice is liked by numerous individuals in the area.

- Southern Thai cooking is the most standard and traditional style for cooking in Thailand since that is the essential tourist territory of the country. In southern cooking, there is significantly more use of coconut milk in various dishes. Coconut replaces Ghee for fricasseeing, and there is a significant usage of fish in majority of their dishes.

- The cooking in northern Thailand is ordinarily milder than in the rest of the country. Firm rice is liked, usually it is kneaded into little balls with the fingers and this is one of the most traditional dishes of Thailand.

- The food in the north east is affected by Laos. The food is astoundingly spiced, and tenacious glutinous rice is the supported staple for north-eastern dishes. Regardless of the point that there are great deals of meat dishes in this section of Thailand, meat was inadequate in these towns, and the highest of protein were shrimp and freshwater fish.

1.3 Evolution of Thai Food over Time

Customarily, while Thai cooking, you do not have to think much as there are a variety of foods available. Thus, arranging food requires heaps of interest and participation, including the family members to cook it all together. The food explains the Thai life and its traditions, customs, and culture. Thai families are gigantic and well-weave. In cooking, Thai family members help each other as a group. In cooking curries, young people assist with light work like nipping off basil leaves, and adults help in pounding chilies and other flavors.

In the current day, making Thai food is much less difficult as each of the ingredients are expeditiously open in general stores, yet there is an examination that it does not have the standard principles of the past.

1.4 Thai Foods According to Nutrition and Dietetics

Thai food is normally adored in the United States, and this food has some amazing nutritional benefits as well. The traditional eating routine of Thailand features striking vegetables, fish, and meats that are given rice or noodles and arranged with flavors like turmeric, galangal, Thai basil, and lemongrass. Food served at Western Thai eateries shares numerous parts of valid Thai cooking, despite the fact that it has some striking contrasts.

Thai menus in America may have greater fragments, more singed nourishments, and plans that are higher in salt and sugar. Following are the curative advantages of Thai food:

- The most generally utilized veggies in Thai dinners are flavorful, like peppers, tomato, cabbage, broccoli, carrots, and onions. These veggies are stacked with fiber, nutrients, minerals, and an assortment of mixtures that add to great absorption and general wellbeing.

- Several of the most well-known Thai ingredients are nutritious, yet there are other sound parts of Thai food. For one, Thai suppers frequently highlight a decent equilibrium of macronutrients like protein, fats, and carbs.

- Eating dinners which to a great extent involve non-bland veggies and furthermore contain protein and fat can assist you with keeping up stable glucose levels for the whole day. This, thusly, prompts supported energy and may help weight reduction.

- Curries, pan-sears, and soups are made with an assortment of vegetables, incorporate a protein source like tofu, lean meat, or fish, and contain coconut milk, nut sauces, or other good fats.

Thai food is known for joining provincial spices and flavors, vegetables, and lean proteins that add both flavor and nourishments to suppers. Nonetheless, some Westernized Thai dishes are pan fried, served in segments, or contain unreasonable measures of added sugar and salt. To pick a solid Thai feast, decide on a dish that are stacked with plant food varieties, contains a protein source, and highlights an assortment of spices and flavors.

1.5 Key Ingredients Used in Thai Food

A large portion of the ingredients found in Thai food are a clear reflection of the environment warm, fertile land and abundant water.

Recipes contain fish, unusual products of the soil, a few sorts of noodles and sauces. Rice is the mainstay of most meals.

Hot flavoring mixes are utilized to season everything from the day's catch to the easy to make servings of rice or noodles. Following are a portion of the primary ingredients utilized in Thai cooking:

- Cumin: Thai cooks broil fragrant, natural cumin seeds in a dry container to draw out its flavor, and afterward granulate it for use in curry pastes and other zest mixes. Cumin is likewise an essential fixing in many flavor mixes, soups, stews, meat, bean and rice dishes.

- Basil: Basil is utilized both as an enhancing flavor and a topping in Thai cooking. Small bunch of basils are commonly used in soups, curries and sautés.

- Cinnamon: Thai cooks favor Chinese cinnamon, or Cinnamomum cassia, which is better, to some degree spicier, and more uncommon in shading and flavor than Cinnamomum zeylanicum.

- Garlic: Thai cooks use garlic for its health properties, fragrance, and the way that its flavor mixes well with an assortment of different flavors. Garlic is a principle ingredient in the customary Big Four Seasonings Blend, alongside salt, cilantro root, and white peppercorns.

- Cardamom: The fragrant cardamom seedpod is utilized in a couple of Thai dishes of Indian inception, as Mussaman curry. Somewhat lemony, cardamom additionally has a marginally peppery and sweet taste as well as fragrance. Thai cooks frequently consolidate cardamom with other sweet-smelling flavors, similar to cinnamon, nutmeg, and mace.

- Lemongrass: The light, lemony flavor and aroma of lemongrass is an important staple in Thai food. Thai cooks utilize the bulb and base leaves of lemongrass to prepare sauces, soups, pan-sears and curries. It improves meats, poultry, fish, and vegetables, and it is particularly delectable with garlic, chilies and cilantro.

- Turmeric: The robes of Buddhist priests in Thailand are shaded with antiquated yellow color produced using turmeric. Its flavor is sweet, warm, and somewhat peppery. However, it is utilized principally for shading in numerous Thai dishes, including curries, toppings, fish and grain dishes.

- Curry Powders and Pastes: Thais generally mix their own curry powders and pastes by pounding different spices and flavors in a mortar and pestle. Curries are utilized to season coconut milk, serving of mixed greens dressings, noodle sauces, fish and meat dishes, vegetable dishes and soups.

- Chili peppers: Thai food is hot, because of its liberal utilization of new and dried stew peppers. Despite the fact that stew peppers are not local, they are presently fundamental for Thai food.

- Coriander: The strongly fragrant and somewhat interesting kind of coriander seeds is valued in Thai cooking. Thai cooks utilize the root and the leaf of the plant.

- Galangal: A relative of ginger, this light yellow zest has a sharp, lemony, peppery hot taste. It is otherwise called galingale, Java root, or Siamese ginger. Enormous, slim bits of galangal are utilized to season Thai soups, stews and curries; for pastes, it is finely sliced and beat. Ginger might be a replacement for galangal in most Thai plans.

- Mace: It has somewhat nutty, warm taste and found in soups, stuffing, sauces and heated products. It supplements fish, meats, and cheddar, just as certain refreshments.

- Cilantro: Also known as Chinese parsley, Thais utilize this delicate, verdant plant for its unmistakable flavor and natural or amazing fragrance.

- Nutmeg: Thai cooks appreciate the extreme fragrance and sweet, zesty kind of nutmeg in recipes for sweet and appetizing dishes. The chefs utilize a grater to finely powder the nutmeg.

- Cloves: This dim earthy colored, sweet-smelling zest is utilized in the Thai kitchen. Its taste is particular, sharp, and warm or sweet, and you will discover it in both sweet and savory plans.

Thai food will engage any cook who adores the art of seasoning. And while many dishes are very hot, those prepared at home can be adjusted to just the right degree for your own tastes.

Chapter 2: The World of Traditional Thai Breakfast Recipes

Following are some classic traditional Thai breakfast recipes that are rich in healthy nutrients and you can easily make them with the detailed instructions list in each recipe:

2.1 Salapao Recipe

Preparation Time: 30 minutes

Cooking Time: 15 minutes

Serving: 4

Ingredients:

- Sugar, half tablespoon
- Ground pork, half pound
- Soy sauce, one tablespoon
- Finely chopped shallots, one tablespoon
- Chopped garlic, half tablespoon
- Thai pepper powder, half teaspoon

For the dough:

- Vegetable oil, one tablespoon
- Milk, one cup
- Mixed flour, one and a half cup
- Sugar, four tablespoon

Instructions:

1. Take a large bowl.
2. Add the mixed flour and sugar.
3. In a separate bowl, add vegetable oil and the milk.
4. Add the dry ingredients into the wet ingredients.
5. Knead the dough until it turns semi soft.
6. In a pan, add the ground pork.
7. Cook your pork and then add the finely chopped shallots.
8. Cook your pork until the color of the pork changes.
9. Once the color changes, add the soy sauce, sugar, Thai pepper powder and the chopped garlic.
10. Once the pork is done, knead the dough into small round buns.
11. Add the ground pork into the buns and cover the buns all over.
12. Place the buns in the steamer and steam your buns.
13. Steam your buns for ten to fifteen minutes.
14. Your dish is ready to be served.

2.2 Khao Neow Sang Kaya Recipe

Preparation Time: 30 minutes

Cooking Time: 10 minutes

Serving: 4

Ingredients:

- Coconut cream, one cup
- Vanilla extract, one teaspoon
- Eggs, four
- Palm sugar, half cup
- Coconut milk, one cup

Instructions:

1. In a large bowl, add eggs and beat them well.
2. Beat the eggs until it forms a foamy structure.
3. Add the coconut cream and vanilla extract.
4. Beat the mixture and form a fluffy mixture.
5. Add the coconut milk and palm sugar.
6. Mix everything well and form a homogenized mixture.
7. Add the mixture into a greased pan.
8. Add the pan into a steamer.
9. Steam your mixture for ten minutes.
10. Dish out your mixture and cut into pieces.
11. Your dish is ready to be served.

2.3 Khanum Pang (Thai Waffles) Recipe

Preparation Time: 30 minutes

Cooking Time: 10 minutes

Serving: 4

Ingredients:

- Rice flour, one cup
- Eggs, two
- Chopped fresh cilantro, half cup
- Coconut milk, one cup
- Salt to taste
- Shredded coconut, half cup
- Cardamom powder, two tablespoon

Instructions:

1. Heat your waffle maker.
2. Always remember you heat your waffle maker till the point that it starts producing steam.
3. Remove the egg whites in a bowl and beat them to the point that they become fluffy.
4. Beat the egg yolks in a separate bowl.
5. Add in the egg yolks in the egg whites and delicately mix them with a spatula.
6. Combine the eggs and the rest of the ingredients.
7. When your waffle maker is heated adequately, pour in the mixture.

8. Close your waffle maker.

9. Let your waffle cook for five to six minutes approximately.

10. When your waffles are done, dish them out.

11. Add on top of the waffles the chopped cilantro leaves.

12. Your dish is ready to be served.

2.4 Khanom Recipe

Preparation Time: 30 minutes

Cooking Time: 25 minutes

Serving: 4

Ingredients:

- Cornstarch, three tablespoon
- Salt, as required
- Fresh chopped chives, two tablespoon
- Full-fat coconut milk, two cups
- Unsweetened shredded coconut, a quarter cup
- Rice flour, two cups
- Sugar, half cup
- White rice (cooked), three tablespoon
- Canola oil, as required

Instructions:

1. In a large bowl add the coconut milk.

2. With the help of an electrical beater, beat the coconut milk for approximately ten minutes.

3. You will see that after ten minutes, the coconut milk would be fluffy.

4. In a grinder, add the white rice and unsweetened shredded coconut.

5. Grind your ingredients into a fine paste without any granules.

6. Now add this mixture into the beaten coconut milk.

7. Fold your mixture well.

8. Add the rice flour, cornstarch and sugar into the mixture.

9. The mixture will become a little heavier but remember not to beat the mixture, rather fold it so the air spaces are kept intact.

10. Mix all the left ingredients into the coconut milk mixture.

11. In a muffin tray, add your coconut milk mixture.

12. Grease the muffin tray with canola oil.

13. Steam your mixture for approximately ten to fifteen minutes.

14. When your khanom is cooked, dish it out.

15. Your dish is ready to be served.

2.5 Khai Luak (Thai Soft Eggs) Recipe

Preparation Time: 30 minutes

Cooking Time: 10 minutes

Serving: 4

Ingredients:

- Vegetable oil, one and a half tablespoon
- Cooked pork chops, one cup
- Eggs, four
- Sliced scallions, four
- Sliced shallots, two medium sized
- Cooked barley, one cup
- Fresh coriander leaves, half cup
- Fish sauce, one tablespoon
- Lime juice, two tablespoon
- Sliced red chili, one long

Instructions:

1. In a medium bowl, mix together the lime juice, fish sauce, one teaspoon of the chili paste, and the cooked grains.

2. Put the eggs and the excess half teaspoon of chili paste in a little bowl.

3. Beat with a fork to mix everything.

4. In a huge weighty sauté dish, heat half tablespoon of the oil over medium-high warmth.

5. Add the shallots, the white areas of the scallions, and the pork, (if utilizing) and cook, blending infrequently, until the shallots are dim earthy colored and withered.

6. Cook for four more minutes.

7. Add the scallion greens and the leftover half tablespoon of oil and cook briefly.

8. Pour in the egg blend and cook for thirty seconds, at that point turn and mix your eggs.

9. Pour in the mixture of the grain and cook, turning with a spatula, until it is cooked properly.

10. Your dish is ready to be served.

2.6 Khao Rad Gyang (Thai Breakfast Rice and Curry) Recipe

Preparation Time: 30 minutes

Cooking Time: 10 minutes

Serving: 4

Ingredients:

- Thai chilies, two
- Jalapeno, one large
- Sliced green onions, half cup
- White peppercorns, one teaspoon
- Cilantro, one cup

- Fresh ginger, one teaspoon
- Fish sauce, one tablespoon
- Soy sauce, one tablespoon
- Chinese 5 spice, half teaspoon
- Chili garlic sauce, two tablespoon
- Fresh cilantro leaves, half cup
- Thai basil leaves, a quarter cup
- Beef broth, one can
- Minced lemon grass, one teaspoon
- Egg, one large
- Cooked rice, as required

Instructions:

1. Add all the ingredients of the curry into a pan.
2. Add the beef broth and sauces into the mixture.
3. Cook your dish for ten minutes.
4. Add the cooked rice into the mixture once the curry is ready.
5. Mix the rice well and cook it for five minutes.
6. Add the egg into the pan by pushing the rest of the ingredients to a side.
7. Cook the egg and then mix the rest of the ingredients into it.
8. Cook your dish for five more minutes.
9. Add the cilantro into the dish.
10. Mix your rice and then dish it out.

11.   Your dish is ready to be served.

2.7 Khao Yum (Thai Breakfast Rice Salad) Recipe

Preparation Time: 10 minutes

Cooking Time: 30 minutes

Serving: 4

Ingredients:

- Water, two tablespoon
- Turmeric powder, one pinch
- Salt to taste
- Garlic cloves, four
- Cooked rice, one cup
- Mix veggies, one cup
- Olive oil

For Thai Dressing:

- Fish sauce, half tablespoon
- Brown sugar, half tablespoon
- Chopped small chili, one
- Water, one tablespoon
- Peanut oil, one teaspoon
- Rice vinegar, half tablespoon
- Sweet chili sauce, half tablespoon

Instructions:

1. Take a large bowl.

2. Add the ingredients for the dressing into the bowl.

3. Mix everything well enough to form a homogeneous mixture.

4. In the next bowl, add the ingredients for the salad.

5. Add the ingredients for the salad into a pan.

6. Cook your ingredients for five to ten minutes.

7. Add the ingredients into a bowl.

8. Add the dressing on top and mix all the ingredients well.

9. Your dish is ready to be served.

2.8 Thai Breakfast Rice and Shrimp Soup Recipe

Preparation Time: 30 minutes

Cooking Time: 10 minutes

Serving: 4

Ingredients:

- White peppercorns, one teaspoon
- Cilantro, one cup
- Shrimps, 150 grams
- Fish sauce, one tablespoon
- Soy sauce, one and a half tablespoon

- Pork stock, three cup
- Jasmine rice, four cups
- Garlic cloves, four

Instructions:

1. Crush the white peppercorns until they turn into powdered form.
2. At that point, add garlic and cilantro and pound until they are crushed.
3. Add portion of this paste to your shrimps and blend well.
4. Sauté the shrimps in a dish with a drop of oil just until it is cooked through.
5. Deglaze the container with some stock and scratch any pieces of spice adhered to the base.
6. Remove from skillet.
7. Bring the stock to a bubble in a pot, add the other portion of the spice paste and stew briefly.
8. Season with fish sauce and soy sauce, at that point taste and add more if you prefer.
9. When prepared to serve, heat the stock to the point of boiling.
10. Add the rice and the shrimp into the stock.
11. Add the soup into a bowl.
12. Garnish it with cilantro leaves.
13. Your dish is ready to be served.

2.9 Thai Styled Traditional Omelet Recipe

Preparation Time: 30 minutes

Cooking Time: 10 minutes

Serving: 4

Ingredients:

- Bean sprouts, one cup
- Fresh coriander leaves, half cup
- Fish sauce, one tablespoon
- Lime juice, two tablespoon
- Sliced red chili, one long
- Green beans, one cup
- Vegetable oil, one and a half tablespoon
- Sliced mushrooms, one cup
- Eggs, eight
- Sliced red capsicum, one large
- Chopped tomatoes, two medium sized

Instructions:

1. Beat the eggs, quarter cup water, lime juice, fish sauce and a large portion of the chili in an enormous container.

2. Heat two teaspoons of oil in a medium non-stick skillet over medium-high warmth.

3. Cook capsicum and mushrooms, mix, for five minutes or until brilliant and delicate.

4. Add the tomatoes.

5. Cook, mixing, for two minutes or until marginally softened.

6. Boil your green beans in water and then drain them.

7. Combine the mushroom blend, sprouts and beans in a bowl.

8. Warm one teaspoon of residual oil in skillet over medium-high heat.

9. Pour quarter of the egg blend into a dish.

10. Cook for thirty seconds or until just set.

11. Slide the omelet onto a plate.

12. Cover your egg to keep it warm.

13. Garnish by sprinkling with coriander and chili.

14. Your dish is ready to be served.

2.10 Thai Breakfast Ginger and Rice Soup Recipe

Preparation Time: 30 minutes

Cooking Time: 10 minutes

Serving: 4

Ingredients:

- White peppercorns, one teaspoon
- Cilantro, one cup
- Ginger paste, two tablespoon
- Fish sauce, one tablespoon
- Soy sauce, one and a half tablespoon
- Pork stock, three cup
- Jasmine rice, four cups
- Garlic cloves, four

Instructions:

1. Crush the white peppercorns until they turn into powdered form.
2. At that point add garlic and cilantro and pound until they are crushed.
3. Add portion of this paste to your ginger paste and blend well.
4. Bring the stock to a bubble in a pot, add the other portion of the spice paste and stew briefly.
5. Season with fish sauce and soy sauce, at that point taste and add more if you prefer.
6. When prepared to serve, heat the stock to the point of boiling.
7. Add the rice and the ginger paste into the stock.
8. Add the soup into a bowl.
9. Garnish it with cilantro leaves.
10. Your dish is ready to be served.

2.11 Spicy Thai Breakfast Noodles Recipe

Preparation Time: 30 minutes

Cooking Time: 10 minutes

Serving: 4

Ingredients:

- Thai chilies, two
- Jalapeno, one large
- Sliced green onions, half cup
- White peppercorns, one teaspoon
- Cilantro, one cup
- Fresh ginger, one teaspoon
- Fish sauce, one tablespoon
- Soy sauce, one tablespoon
- Chinese 5 spice, half teaspoon
- Chili garlic sauce, two tablespoon
- Fresh cilantro leaves, half cup
- Thai basil leaves, a quarter cup
- Beef broth, one can
- Minced lemon grass, one teaspoon
- Egg, one large
- Cooked noodles, as required

Instructions:

1. Add all the ingredients of the sauce into a pan.
2. Add the beef broth and sauces into the mixture.
3. Cook your dish for ten minutes.
4. Add the cooked noodles into the mixture once the sauce is ready.
5. Mix the noodles well and cook it for five minutes.
6. Add the egg into the pan by pushing the rest of the ingredients to a side.
7. Cook the egg and then mix the rest of the ingredients into it.
8. Cook your dish for five more minutes.
9. Add the cilantro into the dish.
10. Mix your noodles and then dish it out.
11. Your dish is ready to be served.

2.12 Thai Fried Eggs Recipe

Preparation Time: 30 minutes

Cooking Time: 10 minutes

Serving: 4

Ingredients:

- Spring onions, four

- Tortilla, as required
- Pepper to taste
- Butter, as required
- Salt to taste
- Baby plum tomatoes, four
- Eggs, four
- Cilantro, half cup

Instructions:

1. Put the butter in a pan.
2. Add the spring onions and chili into the small pan.
3. Cook for a couple of minutes until softened.
4. Whisk the milk and eggs in a bowl.
5. Add the eggs to the pan.
6. Fry your eggs.
7. Add the tomatoes and coriander leaves on top.
8. Once cooked, dish it out.
9. Your dish is ready to be served.

Chapter 3: The World of Traditional Thai Lunch Recipes

Following are some classic traditional Thai lunch recipes that are rich in healthy nutrients and you can easily make them with the detailed instructions list in each recipe:

3.1 Thai Coconut and Noodle Soup Recipe

Preparation Time: 30 minutes

Cooking Time: 10 minutes

Serving: 4

Ingredients:

- Galangal, one can
- Chicken stock, two cups
- Minced garlic, one teaspoon
- Palm sugar, two tablespoon
- Shallot, one
- Kaffir lime leaves, four
- Lime wedges
- Lemon grass, two sticks
- Fish sauce, two tablespoon
- Mushrooms, one cup
- Coconut milk, one cup
- Cilantro, a quarter cup

- Noodles, half pound
- Olive oil, one tablespoon

Instructions:
1. Take a large sauce pan.
2. Add the shallots and olive oil.
3. Cook your shallots and then add the mushrooms.
4. When the mushrooms are cooked then add the galangal, chicken stock, and minced garlic.
5. Add the palm sugar and coconut milk.
6. Cook your ingredients until it starts boiling.
7. Add in the noodles, lemon grass and rest of the ingredients into your soup.
8. Cook your ingredients for ten minutes.
9. When your noodles are cooked dish out your soup.
10. Garnish it with cilantro leaves.
11. Your dish is ready to be served.

3.2 Thai Curry Mud Crab Recipe

Preparation Time: 30 minutes

Cooking Time: 10 minutes

Serving: 4

Ingredients:

- Galangal, one can
- Chicken stock, two cups
- Minced garlic, one teaspoon
- Minced ginger, one teaspoon
- Palm sugar, two tablespoon
- Shallot, one
- Kaffir lime leaves, four
- Lime wedges
- Lemon grass, two sticks
- Fish sauce, two tablespoon
- Mix vegetables, one cup
- Coconut milk, one cup
- Cilantro, a quarter cup
- Crab meat, half pound
- Olive oil, one tablespoon

Instructions:

1. Take a large sauce pan.
2. Add the shallots and olive oil.
3. Cook your shallots and then add the vegetables.
4. When the vegetables are cooked then add the galangal, chicken stock, minced garlic and ginger.
5. Add the palm sugar and coconut milk.
6. Cook your ingredients until it starts boiling.

7. Add in the crab meat, lemon grass and rest of the ingredients into your curry.

8. Cook your ingredients for ten minutes.

9. When your crab meat is cooked dish out your curry.

10.   Garnish it with cilantro leaves.

11.   Your dish is ready to be served.

3.3 Thai Chicken and Sweet Potato Soup Recipe

Preparation Time: 30 minutes

Cooking Time: 10 minutes

Serving: 4

Ingredients:

- Galangal, one can
- Chicken stock, two cups
- Minced garlic, one teaspoon
- Palm sugar, two tablespoon
- Shallot, one
- Kaffir lime leaves, four
- Lime wedges
- Lemon grass, two sticks
- Fish sauce, two tablespoon
- Sweet potatoes, one cup
- Coconut milk, one cup

- Cilantro, a quarter cup
- Chicken meat, half pound
- Olive oil, one tablespoon

Instructions:

1. Take a large sauce pan.
2. Add the shallots and olive oil.
3. Cook your shallots and then add the chicken meat.
4. When the chicken meat is half cooked, add the galangal, chicken stock, and minced garlic.
5. Add the palm sugar and coconut milk.
6. Cook your ingredients until it starts boiling.
7. Add in the sweet potato, lemon grass and rest of the ingredients into your soup.
8. Cook your ingredients for ten minutes.
9. When your sweet potatoes are cooked dish out your soup.
10. Garnish it with cilantro leaves.
11. Your dish is ready to be served.

3.4 Thai Pork and Peanut Curry Recipe

Preparation Time: 30 minutes

Cooking Time: 10 minutes

Serving: 4

Ingredients:

- Galangal, one can
- Chicken stock, two cups
- Minced garlic, one teaspoon
- Minced ginger, one teaspoon
- Chopped onion, half cup
- Kaffir lime leaves, four
- Minced ginger, half tablespoon
- Lemon grass, two sticks
- Fish sauce, two tablespoon
- Peanuts, one cup
- Coconut milk, one cup
- Cilantro, a quarter cup
- Pork meat, half pound
- Olive oil, one tablespoon

Instructions:

1. Take a large sauce pan.
2. Add the chopped onion and olive oil.
3. Cook your chopped onion and then add the pork meat.
4. When the pork meat is half cooked then add the galangal, chicken stock, minced garlic and ginger.
5. Add the coconut milk.
6. Cook your ingredients until it starts boiling.
7. Add in the peanuts, lemon grass and rest of the ingredients into your curry.
8. Cook your ingredients for ten minutes.
9. When the pork meat is cooked completely, dish out your curry.
10. Garnish it with cilantro leaves.
11. Your dish is ready to be served.

3.5 Thai Beef Stir-Fry Recipe

Preparation Time: 10 minutes

Cooking Time: 20 minutes

Serving: 4

Ingredients:

- Fish sauce, two tablespoon
- Soy sauce, half cup

- Beef pieces, three cups
- Tomatoes, two
- Cilantro, half cup
- Salt and pepper, to taste
- Minced ginger, half tablespoon
- Vegetable oil, two tablespoon
- Thai chili peppers, three
- Toasted nuts, half cup
- Onion, one
- Scallions, half cup
- Minced garlic, one teaspoon

Instructions:

1. In a large sauce pan add the shallots and oil.
2. Cook your shallots and then add the ginger and garlic.
3. Cook your ginger and garlic and then add in the beef pieces.
4. Stir fry your beef pieces well.
5. Add all the spices and the rest of the ingredients into your dish except the toasted nuts.
6. When your beef is cooked then add the toasted nuts.
7. Cook your dish for five minutes.
8. Garnish your dish with cilantro.
9. Your dish is ready to be served.

3.6 Thai Minced Chicken Salad Recipe

Preparation Time: 10 minutes

Cooking Time: 20 minutes

Serving: 4

Ingredients:

- Water, two tablespoon
- Turmeric powder, one pinch
- Salt to taste
- Garlic cloves, four
- Cooked chicken mince, one cup
- Olive oil

For Thai Dressing:

- Fish sauce, half tablespoon
- Brown sugar, half tablespoon
- Chopped small chili, one
- Water, one tablespoon
- Peanut oil, one teaspoon
- Rice vinegar, half tablespoon
- Sweet chili sauce, half tablespoon

Instructions:

1. Take a large bowl.
2. Add the ingredients for the dressing into the bowl.
3. Mix everything well enough to form a consistent mixture.
4. In the next bowl, add the ingredients for the salad.
5. Add the ingredients for the salad into a pan.
6. Cook your ingredients for five to ten minutes.
7. Add the ingredients into a bowl.
8. Add the dressing on top and mix all the ingredients well.
9. Your dish is ready to be served.

3.7 Thai Lemongrass Beef Stew with Noodles Recipe

Preparation Time: 30 minutes

Cooking Time: 10 minutes

Serving: 4

Ingredients:

- Galangal, one can
- Beef stock, two cups
- Minced garlic, one teaspoon
- Palm sugar, two tablespoon
- Shallot, one

- Ginger pieces, a quarter cup
- Beef pieces, half pound
- Kaffir lime leaves, four
- Lemon grass, two sticks
- Fish sauce, two tablespoon
- Mixed vegetables, one cup
- Coconut milk, one cup
- Cilantro, a quarter cup
- Noodles, half pound
- Olive oil, one tablespoon

Instructions:

1. Take a large sauce pan.
2. Add the shallots and olive oil.
3. Cook your shallots and then add the mixed vegetables.
4. When the vegetables are cooked then add the galangal, beef stock, and minced garlic.
5. Add the ginger pieces and coconut milk.
6. Cook your ingredients until it starts boiling.
7. Add in the noodles, lemon grass and rest of the ingredients into your soup.
8. Cook your ingredients for ten minutes.
9. When your noodles are cooked dish out your soup.
10. Garnish it with cilantro leaves.
11. Your dish is ready to be served.

3.8 Thai Butternut Squash Soup Recipe

Preparation Time: 30 minutes

Cooking Time: 10 minutes

Serving: 4

Ingredients:

- Galangal, one can
- vegetables stock, two cups
- Minced garlic, one teaspoon
- Palm sugar, two tablespoon
- Shallot, one
- Ginger pieces, a quarter cup
- Butternut squash, half pound
- Kaffir lime leaves, four
- Lemon grass, two sticks
- Fish sauce, two tablespoon
- Coconut milk, one cup
- Cilantro, a quarter cup
- Noodles, half pound
- Olive oil, one tablespoon

Instructions:

1. Take a large sauce pan.

2. Add the shallots and olive oil.

3. Cook your shallots and then add the butternut squash.

4. When the squash is cooked then add the galangal, vegetable stock, and minced garlic.

5. Add the ginger pieces and coconut milk.

6. Cook your ingredients until it starts boiling.

7. Add in the lemon grass and rest of the ingredients into your soup.

8. Cook your ingredients for ten minutes.

9. Garnish it with cilantro leaves.

10. Your dish is ready to be served.

3.9 Thai Green Chicken Soup Recipe

Preparation Time: 30 minutes

Cooking Time: 10 minutes

Serving: 4

Ingredients:

- Galangal, one can
- Chicken stock, two cups
- Minced garlic, one teaspoon
- Palm sugar, two tablespoon

- Shallot, one
- Kaffir lime leaves, four
- Lime wedges
- Lemon grass, two sticks
- Fish sauce, two tablespoon
- Thai green curry paste, two tablespoon
- Coconut milk, one cup
- Cilantro, a quarter cup
- Chicken meat, half pound
- Olive oil, one tablespoon

Instructions:

1. Take a large sauce pan.
2. Add the shallots and olive oil.
3. Cook your shallots and then add the chicken meat.
4. When the chicken meat is half cooked, add the galangal, green curry paste, chicken stock, and minced garlic.
5. Add the palm sugar and coconut milk.
6. Cook your ingredients until it starts boiling.
7. Add in the lemon grass and rest of the ingredients into your soup.
8. Cook your ingredients for ten minutes.
9. When your chicken meat is cooked completely, dish out your soup.
10. Garnish it with cilantro leaves.

11.   Your dish is ready to be served.

3.10 Thai Baked Chicken and Rice Recipe

Preparation Time: 30 minutes

Cooking Time: 25 minutes

Serving: 4

Ingredients:

- Minced ginger, two tablespoon
- Cilantro, half cup
- Olive oil, two tablespoon
- Chopped tomatoes, one cup
- Powdered cumin, one tablespoon
- Salt, to taste
- Black pepper, to taste
- Turmeric powder, one teaspoon
- Fresh Thai herbs, two tablespoon
- Onion, one cup
- Smoked paprika, half teaspoon
- Whole chicken, one pound
- Minced garlic, two tablespoon
- Cooked jasmine rice, as required

Instructions:

1. Take a pan.
2. Add in the oil and onions.
3. Cook the onions until they become soft and fragrant.
4. Add in the chopped garlic and ginger.
5. Cook the mixture and add the tomatoes into it.
6. Add the spices.
7. When the tomatoes are done, add the chicken into it.
8. Mix the chicken so that the tomatoes and spices are coated all over the chicken.
9. Place the chicken on a baking tray and cover your chicken with aluminum foil.
10. Place fresh Thai herbs in the chicken.
11. Bake your chicken for fifteen to twenty minutes.
12. When your chicken is done, dish it out.
13. Sprinkle the cilantro on top of the chicken.
14. Cut your chicken into pieces and place it on the jasmine rice.
15. Your dish is ready to be served.

3.11 Thai Pork Belly with Basil and Tofu Recipe

Preparation Time: 30 minutes

Cooking Time: 10 minutes

Serving: 4

Ingredients:

- Thai chilies, two
- Jalapeno, one large
- Sliced green onions, half cup
- Pork belly pieces, two cups
- Tofu cubes, two cups
- White peppercorns, one teaspoon
- Cilantro, one cup
- Fresh ginger, one teaspoon
- Fish sauce, one tablespoon
- Soy sauce, one tablespoon
- Chinese 5 spice, half teaspoon
- Chili garlic sauce, two tablespoon
- Fresh cilantro leaves, half cup
- Thai basil leaves, a quarter cup
- Chicken broth, one can
- Minced lemon grass, one teaspoon

Instructions:

1. Add all the ingredients of the sauce into a pan.
2. Add the chicken broth and sauces into the mixture.
3. Cook your dish for ten minutes.
4. Add the pork belly pieces and tofu pieces into the mixture once the sauce is ready.

5. Mix the ingredients well and cook it for five minutes.

6. Add the basil leaves and then mix the rest of the ingredients into it.

7. Cook your dish for five more minutes.

8. Add the cilantro into the dish.

9. Your dish is ready to be served.

3.12 Thai Red Meatball Curry Recipe

Preparation Time: 30 minutes

Cooking Time: 10 minutes

Serving: 4

Ingredients:

- Galangal, one can
- Chicken stock, two cups
- Minced garlic, one teaspoon
- Palm sugar, two tablespoon
- Shallot, one
- Kaffir lime leaves, four
- Lime wedges
- Lemon grass, two sticks
- Fish sauce, two tablespoon
- Thai red curry paste, two tablespoon
- Coconut milk, one cup

- Cilantro, a quarter cup
- Frozen meatballs, half pound
- Olive oil, one tablespoon

Instructions:

1. Take a large sauce pan.
2. Add the shallots and olive oil.
3. Cook your shallots and then add the meatballs.
4. When the meatballs are half cooked, add the galangal, red curry paste, chicken stock, and minced garlic.
5. Add the palm sugar and coconut milk.
6. Cook your ingredients until it starts boiling.
7. Add in the lemon grass and rest of the ingredients into the curry.
8. Cook your ingredients for ten minutes.
9. When your curry is cooked dish it out.
10. Garnish it with cilantro leaves.
11. Your dish is ready to be served.

3.13 Thai Sesame Chicken Salad Recipe

Preparation Time: 10 minutes

Cooking Time: 20 minutes

Serving: 4

Ingredients:

- White sesame seeds, half cup
- Black sesame seeds, half cup
- Salt to taste
- Garlic cloves, four
- Cooked chicken meat, one cup
- Olive oil

For Thai Dressing:

- Fish sauce, half tablespoon
- Brown sugar, half tablespoon
- Chopped small chili, one
- Water, one tablespoon
- Peanut oil, one teaspoon
- Rice vinegar, half tablespoon
- Sweet chili sauce, half tablespoon

Instructions:

1. Take a large bowl.
2. Add the ingredients for the dressing into the bowl.
3. Mix everything well enough to form a smooth mixture.
4. In the next bowl, add the ingredients for the salad.
5. Add the ingredients for the salad into a bowl.

6. Add the dressing on top and mix all the ingredients well.

7. Your dish is ready to be served.

3.14 Spicy Thai Prawn Noodles Recipe

Preparation Time: 30 minutes

Cooking Time: 10 minutes

Serving: 4

Ingredients:

- Thai chilies, two
- Jalapeno, one large
- Sliced green onions, half cup
- White peppercorns, one teaspoon
- Cilantro, one cup
- Fresh ginger, one teaspoon
- Fish sauce, one tablespoon
- Soy sauce, one tablespoon
- Chinese 5 spice, half teaspoon
- Chili garlic sauce, two tablespoon
- Fresh cilantro leaves, half cup
- Prawns, two cups
- Fish broth, one can
- Minced lemon grass, one teaspoon
- Cooked noodles, as required

Instructions:

1. Add all the ingredients of the sauce into a pan.
2. Add the fish broth and sauces into the mixture.
3. Cook your dish for ten minutes.
4. Add the cooked noodles into the mixture once the sauce is ready.
5. Mix the noodles well and cook it for five minutes.
6. Add the prawns into the pan by pushing the rest of the ingredients to a side.
7. Cook the prawns and then mix the rest of the ingredients into it.
8. Cook your dish for five more minutes.
9. Add the cilantro into the dish.
10. Mix your noodles and then dish it out.
11. Your dish is ready to be served.

3.15 Thai Red Salmon Curry Recipe

Preparation Time: 30 minutes

Cooking Time: 10 minutes

Serving: 4

Ingredients:

- Galangal, one can
- Fish stock, two cups
- Minced garlic, one teaspoon
- Shallot, one

- Kaffir lime leaves, four
- Lemon grass, two sticks
- Fish sauce, two tablespoon
- Thai red curry paste, two tablespoon
- Cilantro, a quarter cup
- Salmon meat, half pound
- Olive oil, one tablespoon

Instructions:

1. Take a large sauce pan.
2. Add the shallots and olive oil.
3. Cook your shallots and then add the salmon meat.
4. When the salmon meat is half cooked, add the galangal, red curry paste, fish stock, and minced garlic.
5. Cook your ingredients until it starts boiling.
6. Add in the lemon grass and rest of the ingredients into the curry.
7. Cook your ingredients for ten minutes.
8. When your curry is cooked dish it out.
9. Garnish it with cilantro leaves.
10. Your dish is ready to be served.

Chapter 4: The World of Traditional Thai Dinner Recipes

Following are some classic traditional Thai dinner recipes that are rich in healthy nutrients and you can easily make them with the detailed instructions list in each recipe:

4.1 Thai Peanut Chicken and Noodles Recipe

Preparation Time: 30 minutes

Cooking Time: 10 minutes

Serving: 4

Ingredients:

- Galangal, one can
- Chicken stock, two cups
- Minced garlic, one teaspoon
- Minced ginger, one teaspoon
- Chopped onion, half cup
- Noodles, two cups
- Minced ginger, half tablespoon
- Lemon grass, two sticks
- Fish sauce, two tablespoon
- Peanuts, one cup
- Coconut milk, one cup

- Cilantro, a quarter cup
- Chicken meat, half pound
- Olive oil, one tablespoon

Instructions:

1. Take a large sauce pan.
2. Add the chopped onion and olive oil.
3. Cook your chopped onion and then add the chicken meat.
4. When the chicken meat is half cooked then add the galangal, chicken stock, minced garlic and ginger.
5. Add the coconut milk.
6. Cook your ingredients until it starts boiling.
7. Add in the noodles, peanuts, lemon grass and rest of the ingredients into your curry.
8. Cook your ingredients for ten minutes.
9. Garnish it with cilantro leaves.
10. Your dish is ready to be served.

4.2 Thai Red Curry Chicken and Vegetable Recipe

Preparation Time: 30 minutes

Cooking Time: 10 minutes

Serving: 4

Ingredients:

- Galangal, one can
- Chicken stock, two cups
- Minced garlic, one teaspoon
- Shallot, one
- Mix vegetables, one cup
- Lemon grass, two sticks
- Fish sauce, two tablespoon
- Thai red curry paste, two tablespoon
- Cilantro, a quarter cup
- Chicken meat, half pound
- Olive oil, one tablespoon

Instructions:

1. Take a large sauce pan.
2. Add the shallots and olive oil.
3. Cook your shallots and then add the chicken meat and vegetables.
4. When the chicken meat is half cooked, add the galangal, red curry paste, chicken stock, and minced garlic.
5. Cook your ingredients until it starts boiling.
6. Add in the lemon grass and rest of the ingredients into the dish.
7. Cook your ingredients for ten minutes.

8. Garnish it with cilantro leaves.

9. Your dish is ready to be served.

4.3 Thai Noodles with Spicy Peanut Sauce Recipe

Preparation Time: 30 minutes

Cooking Time: 10 minutes

Serving: 4

Ingredients:

- Mixed vegetables, two cups
- Minced garlic, one teaspoon
- Minced ginger, one teaspoon
- Chopped onion, half cup
- Noodles, two cups
- Minced ginger, half tablespoon
- Lemon grass, two sticks
- Fish sauce, two tablespoon
- Spicy peanut sauce, one cup
- Coconut milk, one cup
- Cilantro, a quarter cup
- Olive oil, one tablespoon

Instructions:

1. Take a large sauce pan.

2. Add the chopped onion and olive oil.

3. Cook your chopped onion and then add the vegetables.

4. Add the coconut milk.

5. Cook your ingredients until it starts boiling.

6. Add in the noodles, spicy peanut sauce and the rest of the ingredients.

7. Cook your ingredients for ten minutes.

8. Garnish it with cilantro leaves.

9. Your dish is ready to be served.

4.4 Thai Coconut and Beef Curry Recipe

Preparation Time: 30 minutes

Cooking Time: 10 minutes

Serving: 4

Ingredients:

- Galangal, one can
- Beef stock, two cups
- Minced garlic, one teaspoon
- Crushed ginger, one teaspoon
- Chopped onion, half cup
- Minced ginger, half tablespoon
- Lemon grass, two sticks

- Fish sauce, two tablespoon
- Shredded coconut, one cup
- Coconut milk, one cup
- Cilantro, a quarter cup
- Beef meat, half pound
- Olive oil, one tablespoon

Instructions:

1. Take a large sauce pan.
2. Add the chopped onion and olive oil.
3. Cook your chopped onion and then add the beef meat.
4. When the beef meat is half cooked then add the galangal, beef stock, minced garlic and ginger.
5. Add the coconut milk.
6. Cook your ingredients until it starts boiling.
7. Add in the shredded coconut, lemon grass and rest of the ingredients into your curry.
8. Cook your ingredients for ten minutes.
9. When your beef meat is cooked completely dish out your curry.
10. Garnish it with cilantro leaves.
11. Your dish is ready to be served.

4.5 Thai Coconut and Beef Salad Recipe

Preparation Time: 10 minutes

Cooking Time: 20 minutes

Serving: 4

Ingredients:

- Water, two tablespoon
- Shredded coconut, half cup
- Salt to taste
- Garlic cloves, four
- Cooked beef strips, one cup
- Olive oil

For Thai Dressing:
- Fish sauce, half tablespoon
- Brown sugar, half tablespoon
- Chopped small chili, one
- Water, one tablespoon
- Peanut oil, one teaspoon
- Rice vinegar, half tablespoon
- Sweet chili sauce, half tablespoon

Instructions:
1. Take a large bowl.
2. Add the ingredients for the dressing into the bowl.
3. Mix everything well enough to form a consistent mixture.
4. In the next bowl, add the ingredients for the salad.

5. Add the ingredients for the salad into a bowl and mix properly.

6. Add the dressing on top and mix all the ingredients well.

7. Your dish is ready to be served.

4.6 Thai Green Chicken Thighs Recipe

Preparation Time: 10 minutes

Cooking Time: 40 minutes

Serving: 2

Ingredients:

- Chicken broth, one cup
- Thai green curry paste, one teaspoon
- Onion, one cup
- Lemon juice, half cup
- Chicken thighs, half pound
- Thai spices, half tablespoon
- Water, one cup
- Minced garlic, two tablespoon
- Minced ginger, two tablespoon
- Cilantro, half cup
- Olive oil, two tablespoon

- Chopped tomatoes, one cup

Instructions:

1. Take a pan.
2. Add in the oil and onions.
3. Cook the onions until they become soft and fragrant.
4. Add in the chopped garlic and ginger.
5. Cook the mixture and add the tomatoes into it.
6. Add the spices and chicken thighs.
7. Add in the broth.
8. Mix the ingredients carefully and cover your pan.
9. Add cilantro on top.
10. Your dish is ready to be served.

4.7 Thai Basil Pork Stir-Fry Recipe

Preparation Time: 10 minutes

Cooking Time: 20 minutes

Serving: 4

Ingredients:

- Fish sauce, two tablespoon
- Soy sauce, half cup
- Pork pieces, three cups
- Tomatoes, two

- Cilantro, half cup
- Salt and pepper, to taste
- Minced ginger, half tablespoon
- Vegetable oil, two tablespoon
- Thai chili peppers, three
- Basil leaves, half cup
- Onion, one
- Minced garlic, one teaspoon

Instructions:

1. In a large sauce pan, add the onions and oil.
2. Cook your onions and then add the ginger and garlic.
3. Cook your ginger and garlic and then add in the pork pieces.
4. Stir fry your pork pieces well.
5. Add all the spices and the rest of the ingredients into your dish except the basil leaves.
6. When your pork is cooked then add the basil leaves.
7. Cook your dish for five minutes.
8. Garnish your dish with cilantro.
9. Your dish is ready to be served.

4.8 Thai Green Chicken Curry with Vegetables Recipe

Preparation Time: 30 minutes

Cooking Time: 10 minutes

Serving: 4

Ingredients:

- Galangal, one can
- Chicken stock, two cups
- Minced garlic, one teaspoon
- Shallot, one
- Kaffir lime leaves, four
- Lime wedges
- Lemon grass, two sticks
- Fish sauce, two tablespoon
- Thai green curry paste, two tablespoon
- Mixed vegetables, one cup
- Cilantro, a quarter cup
- Chicken pieces, half pound
- Olive oil, one tablespoon

Instructions:

1. Take a large sauce pan.
2. Add the shallots and olive oil.
3. Cook your shallots and then add the chicken pieces and vegetables.
4. When the chicken pieces are half cooked, add the galangal, green curry paste, chicken stock, and minced garlic.
5. Cook your ingredients until it starts boiling.
6. Add in the lemon grass and rest of the ingredients into your soup.
7. Cook your ingredients for ten minutes.
8. When your chicken pieces are cooked completely dish out your soup.
9. Garnish it with cilantro leaves.
10. Your dish is ready to be served.

4.9 Thai Mussels in Basil Coconut Sauce Recipe

Preparation Time: 30 minutes

Cooking Time: 10 minutes

Serving: 4

Ingredients:

- Galangal, one can
- Fish stock, two cups

- Minced garlic, one teaspoon
- Minced ginger, one teaspoon
- Chopped onion, half cup
- Crushed ginger, half tablespoon
- Basil leaves, a quarter cup
- Fish sauce, two tablespoon
- Shredded coconut, one cup
- Coconut milk, one cup
- Cilantro, a quarter cup
- Mussels, half pound
- Olive oil, one tablespoon

Instructions:

1. Take a large sauce pan.
2. Add the chopped onion and olive oil.
3. Cook your chopped onion and then add the mussels.
4. When the mussels are half cooked then add the galangal, fish stock, minced garlic and ginger.
5. Add the coconut milk.
6. Cook your ingredients until it starts boiling.
7. Add in the shredded coconut, basil leaves and rest of the ingredients into your curry.
8. Cook your ingredients for ten minutes.
9. Garnish it with cilantro leaves.
10. Your dish is ready to be served.

4.10 Thai Pumpkin and Sweet Potato Curry Recipe

Preparation Time: 30 minutes

Cooking Time: 10 minutes

Serving: 4

Ingredients:

- Galangal, one can
- Chicken stock, two cups
- Chopped garlic, one teaspoon
- Palm sugar, two tablespoon
- Shallot, one
- Lemon grass, two sticks
- Fish sauce, two tablespoon
- Sweet potatoes, one cup
- Coconut milk, one cup
- Cilantro, a quarter cup
- Pumpkin pieces, two cups
- Olive oil, one tablespoon

Instructions:

1. Take a large sauce pan.

2. Add the shallots and olive oil.

3. Cook your shallots.

4. When the pumpkin and sweet potatoes is half cooked, add the galangal, chicken stock, and minced garlic.

5. Cook your ingredients until it starts boiling.

6. Add in the lemon grass and rest of the ingredients into your curry.

7. Cook your ingredients for ten minutes.

8. Garnish it with cilantro leaves.

9. Your dish is ready to be served.

4.11 Thai Tofu Fried Rice Recipe

Preparation Time: 30 minutes

Cooking Time: 10 minutes

Serving: 4

Ingredients:

- Tofu cubes, one cup
- Jalapeno, one large
- Sliced green onions, half cup
- White peppercorns, one teaspoon
- Cilantro, one cup
- Fresh ginger, one teaspoon
- Fish sauce, one tablespoon
- Soy sauce, one tablespoon

- Chinese 5 spice, half teaspoon
- Chili garlic sauce, two tablespoon
- Fresh cilantro leaves, half cup
- Thai basil leaves, a quarter cup
- Vegetable broth, one can
- Minced lemon grass, one teaspoon
- Cooked rice, as required

Instructions:

1. Add all the ingredients of the curry into a pan.
2. Add the vegetable broth and sauces into the mixture.
3. Cook your dish for ten minutes.
4. Add the cooked rice into the mixture once the curry is ready.
5. Mix the rice well and cook it for five minutes.
6. Add the tofu pieces into the pan by pushing the rest of the ingredients to a side.
7. Cook the tofu pieces and then mix the rest of the ingredients into it.
8. Cook your dish for five more minutes.
9. Add the cilantro into the dish.
10. Mix your rice and then dish it out.
11. Your dish is ready to be served.

4.12 Thai Chicken Pad Thai Recipe

Preparation Time: 30 minutes

Cooking Time: 10 minutes

Serving: 4

Ingredients:

- Mixed vegetables, two cups
- Sliced green onions, half cup
- White peppercorns, one teaspoon
- Cilantro, one cup
- Fresh ginger, one teaspoon
- Fish sauce, one tablespoon
- Soy sauce, one tablespoon
- Chinese 5 spice, half teaspoon
- Chili garlic sauce, two tablespoon
- Fresh cilantro leaves, half cup
- Thai basil leaves, a quarter cup
- Chicken broth, one can
- Chicken pieces, half pound
- Cooked noodles, as required

Instructions:

1. Add all the ingredients of the sauce into a pan.
2. Add the chicken pieces, vegetables, chicken broth and sauces into the mixture.
3. Cook your dish for ten minutes.
4. Add the cooked noodles into the mixture once the sauce is ready.
5. Mix the noodles well and cook it for five minutes.
6. Add the cilantro into the dish.
7. Mix your noodles and then dish it out.
8. Your dish is ready to be served.

4.13 Thai Sour and Spicy Soup Recipe

Preparation Time: 30 minutes

Cooking Time: 10 minutes

Serving: 4

Ingredients:

- Galangal, one can
- Vegetables stock, two cups
- Minced garlic, one teaspoon
- Palm sugar, two tablespoon
- Shallot, one
- Sweet and sour sauce, half cup
- Ginger pieces, a quarter cup

- Lemon grass, two sticks
- Fish sauce, two tablespoon
- Mixed vegetables, one cup
- Coconut milk, one cup
- Cilantro, a quarter cup
- Olive oil, one tablespoon

Instructions:

1. Take a large sauce pan.
2. Add the shallots and olive oil.
3. Cook your shallots and then add the mixed vegetables.
4. When the vegetables are cooked then add the galangal, vegetable stock, and minced garlic.
5. Add the ginger pieces and coconut milk.
6. Cook your ingredients until it starts boiling.
7. Add in the sweet and sour sauce, lemon grass and rest of the ingredients into your soup.
8. Cook your ingredients for ten minutes.
9. Garnish it with cilantro leaves.
10. Your dish is ready to be served.

4.14 Thai Pumpkin and Coconut Curry Recipe

Preparation Time: 30 minutes

Cooking Time: 10 minutes

Serving: 4

Ingredients:

- Galangal, one can
- Vegetable stock, two cups
- Minced garlic, one teaspoon
- Minced ginger, one teaspoon
- Chopped onion, half cup
- Minced ginger, half tablespoon
- Lemon grass, two sticks
- Fish sauce, two tablespoon
- Shredded coconut, one cup
- Coconut milk, one cup
- Cilantro, a quarter cup
- Pumpkin pieces, half pound
- Olive oil, one tablespoon

Instructions:
1. Take a large sauce pan.
2. Add the chopped onion and olive oil.
3. Cook your chopped onion and then add the pumpkin pieces.
4. When the pumpkin pieces are half cooked then add the galangal, vegetable stock, minced garlic and ginger.

5. Add the coconut milk.

6. Add in the shredded coconut, lemon grass and rest of the ingredients into your curry.

7. Cook your ingredients for ten minutes.

8. Garnish it with cilantro leaves.

9. Your dish is ready to be served.

4.15 Thai Grilled Salmon Recipe

Preparation Time: 30 minutes

Cooking Time: 25 minutes

Serving: 4

Ingredients:

- Minced ginger, two tablespoon
- Cilantro, half cup
- Olive oil, two tablespoon
- Chopped tomatoes, one cup
- Powdered cumin, one tablespoon
- Salt, to taste
- Black pepper, to taste
- Turmeric powder, one teaspoon
- Fresh Thai herbs, two tablespoon
- Onion, one cup
- Salmon filet, one pound

- Minced garlic, two tablespoon

Instructions:

1. Take a pan.
2. Add in the oil and onions.
3. Cook the onions until they become soft and fragrant.
4. Add in the chopped garlic and ginger.
5. Cook the mixture and add the tomatoes into it.
6. Add the spices.
7. Mix the salmon so that the tomatoes and spices are coated all over the salmon.
8. Place fresh Thai herbs on the salmon.
9. Grill your salmon for fifteen to twenty minutes.
10. When your salmon is done, dish it out.
11. Sprinkle the cilantro on top of the salmon.
12. Your dish is ready to be served.

4.16 Thai Red Beef Curry Recipe

Preparation Time: 30 minutes

Cooking Time: 10 minutes

Serving: 4

Ingredients:

- Beef stock, two cups
- Crushed garlic, one teaspoon

- Palm sugar, two tablespoon
- Shallot, one
- Kaffir lime leaves, four
- Lemon grass, two sticks
- Fish sauce, two tablespoon
- Thai red curry paste, two tablespoon
- Cilantro, a quarter cup
- Beef, half pound
- Olive oil, one tablespoon

Instructions:

1. Take a large sauce pan.
2. Add the shallots and olive oil.
3. Cook your shallots and then add the beef meat.
4. When the beef is half cooked, add the red curry paste, beef stock, and minced garlic.
5. Cook your ingredients until it starts boiling.
6. Add in the lemon grass and rest of the ingredients into the curry.
7. Cook your ingredients for ten minutes.
8. When your curry is cooked, dish it out.
9. Garnish it with cilantro leaves.
10. Your dish is ready to be served.

4.17 Thai Coconut Curry Recipe

Preparation Time: 30 minutes

Cooking Time: 10 minutes

Serving: 4

Ingredients:

- Galangal, one can
- Vegetable stock, two cups
- Minced garlic, one teaspoon
- Minced ginger, one teaspoon
- Chopped onion, half cup
- Chopped ginger, half tablespoon
- Lemon grass, two sticks
- Fish sauce, two tablespoon
- Shredded coconut, one cup
- Coconut milk, one cup
- Cilantro, a quarter cup
- Olive oil, one tablespoon

Instructions:

1. Take a large sauce pan.
2. Add the chopped onion and olive oil.
3. Cook your chopped onion.

4. When the onions are cooked then add the galangal, vegetable stock, minced garlic and ginger.

5. Add the coconut milk.

6. Cook your ingredients until it starts boiling.

7. Add in the shredded coconut, lemon grass and rest of the ingredients into your curry.

8. Cook your ingredients for ten minutes.

9. Garnish it with cilantro leaves.

10. Your dish is ready to be served.

4.18 Thai Pumpkin and Vegetable Soup Recipe

Preparation Time: 30 minutes

Cooking Time: 10 minutes

Serving: 4

Ingredients:

- Vegetables stock, two cups
- Minced garlic, one teaspoon
- Galangal, one can
- Shallot, one
- Pumpkin pieces, one cup
- Ginger pieces, a quarter cup
- Lemon grass, two sticks
- Fish sauce, two tablespoon

- Mixed vegetables, one cup
- Coconut milk, one cup
- Cilantro, a quarter cup
- Olive oil, one tablespoon

Instructions:

1. Take a large sauce pan.
2. Add the shallots and olive oil.
3. Cook your shallots and then add the mixed vegetables.
4. When the vegetables are cooked then add the galangal, vegetable stock, and minced garlic.
5. Add the ginger pieces and coconut milk.
6. Cook your ingredients until it starts boiling.
7. Add in the pumpkin, lemon grass and rest of the ingredients into your soup.
8. Cook your ingredients for ten minutes.
9. Garnish it with cilantro leaves.
10. Your dish is ready to be served.

Chapter 5: The World of Traditional Thai Dessert Recipes

Following are some classic traditional Thai dessert recipes that are rich in healthy nutrients and you can easily make them with the detailed instructions list in each recipe:

5.1 Thai Coconut Pudding Recipe

Preparation Time: 10 minutes

Cooking Time: 30 minutes

Serving: 2

Ingredients:

- Coconut Milk, two cups
- White sugar, half cup
- Salt, one teaspoon
- Eggs, two
- Lemon extract, one teaspoon
- Almond extract, one teaspoon
- All-purpose flour, two cups
- Butter, one cup
- Dry yeast, one cup

Instructions:

1. Take a medium bowl and add the butter in it.
2. Add one cup flour and mix well.
3. Then refrigerate it.
4. Take a large bowl and add yeast into it.
5. Add the sugar, the salt and the milk.
6. Mix them well.
7. Mix the warm milk mixture with the flour and the yeast.
8. Add the lemon extract, eggs and almond extract together.
9. Add the baking soda in the mixture.
10. Simmer it for few minutes.
11. Check the thickness of the pudding.
12. Serve warm.

5.2 Thai Fruit Salad Recipe

Preparation Time: 10 minutes

Cooking Time: 30 minutes

Serving: 2

Ingredients:

- Bananas, five or six
- Apples, two or three
- Spring onions, three
- Gem lettuce, separated into leaves

- Lime zest, one
- Chili sauce, one teaspoon
- Fish sauce, one tablespoon
- Rice vinegar, one tablespoon
- Sugar, one tablespoon
- Sesame oil, one tablespoon
- Sesame seeds, one cup

Instructions:

1. Take a large bowl to put all the ingredients into it.
2. First of all, slice the bananas into small pieces so that proper mixing can be done.
3. Then slice the apples in the same way.
4. Put them into the bowl.
5. Add chili sauce and fish sauce into the bowl.
6. Add all spices one by one.
7. Add the rice vinegar in such a way equal distribution can be done.
8. Take the gem lettuce in a separate bowl.
9. Add the lime zest and juice into it.
10. Add the spring onions, sesame seeds and sesame oil into it.
11. Mix all the ingredients so that a good paste is formed
12. Then add it in the first bowl with apples and bananas.
13. You can add sugar as per your requirement.

14.   Your salad is ready to be served with chili sauce.

5.3 Thai Mung Bean Pudding Recipe

Preparation Time: 10 minutes

Cooking Time: 15 minutes

Serving: 4

Ingredients:
- Tapioca flour, one cup
- Mung beans, half cup
- Coconut milk, half cup
- White sugar, half cup
- Salt, one teaspoon
- Eggs, two
- Lemon extract, one teaspoon
- Almond extract, one teaspoon
- All-purpose flour, two cups
- Butter, one cup

Instructions:
1. Take a medium bowl and add the mung beans in it.
2. Add one cup tapioca flour and mix well.
3. Then refrigerate it.

4. Take a large bowl and add the coconut milk into it.

5. Add the sugar, salt and milk.

6. Mix them well.

7. Mix the warm milk mixture with the flour and the mung beans.

8. Add the eggs, lemon extract and almond extract together.

9. Add the baking soda in the mixture.

10. Simmer it for few minutes.

11. Check the thickness of the pudding.

12. Your dish is ready to be served.

5.4 Thai Mango Sticky Rice Recipe

Preparation Time: 10 minutes

Cooking Time: 10 minutes

Serving: 4

Ingredients:

- Water, one and a half cup
- Ripe mangoes, two
- Thai sweet rice, one cup
- Coconut milk, one can
- Salt, a quarter teaspoon
- Brown sugar, five tablespoon

Instructions:

1. Add half cup of water, rice, plus half can of the coconut milk, the salt, and one tablespoon of the brown sugar.

2. Stir well.

3. Add coconut milk, salt, and some of the brown sugar to the saucepan.

4. Bring to a gentle boil, and then partially cover with a lid.

5. Reduce heat to medium-low, or just until you get a gentle simmer.

6. Simmer thirty minutes, or until the coconut water has been absorbed by the rice.

7. Turn off the heat but leave the pot on the burner with the lid on it tightly.

8. Allow it to stay for five minutes.

9. To make the sauce, warm the remaining coconut milk over medium-low heat.

10. Add three tablespoons of brown sugar, stirring to dissolve.

11. Prepare the mangoes by cutting them open and slicing each into bite-sized pieces.

12. Scoop some warm rice into each serving bowl, and then drizzle lots of the sweet coconut sauce over the top.

13. Arrange mango slices on the rice and finish with a drizzle of more sauce.

14. Your dish is ready to be served.

5.5 Thai Mango Tapioca Pudding Recipe

Preparation Time: 10 minutes

Cooking Time: 10 minutes

Serving: 4

Ingredients:

- Tapioca flour, one cup
- Mangoes, two
- Coconut milk, half cup
- White sugar, half cup
- Salt, one teaspoon
- Eggs, two
- Lemon extract, one teaspoon
- Almond extract, one teaspoon
- All-purpose flour, two cups
- Butter, one cup

Instructions:

1. Take a medium bowl and add the tapioca flour in it.
2. Add the one cup coconut milk and mix well.
3. Then refrigerate it.

4. Take a large bowl and add the spices into it.

5. Add the sugar, salt and mangoes.

6. Mix them well.

7. Mix the warm milk mixture with the flour and the mangoes.

8. Add the eggs, lemon extract and almond extract together.

9. Add the baking soda in the mixture.

10.   Simmer it for few minutes.

11.   Check the thickness of the pudding.

12.   Your dish is ready to be served.

5.6 Thai Fried Bananas Recipe

Preparation Time: 30 minutes

Cooking Time: 10 minutes

Serving: 4

Ingredients:

- Bananas, five
- Cornstarch, one tablespoon
- Water, two cups
- Coconut milk, one cup
- Rice flour, one cup
- Chinese five spice, as needed
- Cooking oil, as required

Instructions:

1. In a large bowl, add all the ingredients together except the bananas and oil.
2. Mix everything to form a consistent mixture.
3. Dip your bananas into the mixture and then fry them in the cooking oil.
4. Fry your bananas until they turn golden brown.
5. Dish out and drizzle maple syrup if you want on top.
6. Your dish is ready to be served.

5.7 Thai Steamed Banana Cake Recipe

Preparation Time: 10 minutes

Cooking Time: 20 minutes

Serving: 4

Ingredients:

- Bananas, five
- Salt, two tablespoon
- White sugar, two cups
- Cornstarch, one tablespoon
- Water, two cups
- Coconut milk, one cup
- Rice flour, one cup
- Pandan essence, as needed

- Raspberries, aa required

Instructions:

1. Take bananas and peel them.
2. Then steam them properly.
3. Take water in a pot and heat it.
4. Take a large bowl and add the sweet rice into it.
5. Cook the rice and add some of sugar into it for taste.
6. Take another bowl and add coconut milk into it.
7. Mix the palm sugar into the coconut milk.
8. Then mix the rice cooked and coconut milk together.
9. Take them into a large bowl after mixing.
10. Add steamed bananas and raspberries into it.
11. Mix them well and then bake your cake.
12. Your cake is ready to be served.

5.8 Thai Tea Cake Recipe

Preparation Time: 10 minutes

Cooking Time: 40 minutes

Serving: 2

Ingredients:

- Tea, one cup
- Salt, two tablespoon
- White sugar, two cups
- Cornstarch, one tablespoon
- Water, two cups
- Coconut milk, one cup
- Rice flour, one cup
- Pandan essence, as needed
- Raspberries, as required

Instructions:

1. Take one cup of tea.
2. Take water in a pot and heat it.
3. Take a large bowl and add the sweet rice into it.
4. Cook the rice and add some of the sugar into it for taste.
5. Take another bowl and add coconut milk into it.
6. Mix the palm sugar into the coconut milk.
7. Then mix the rice cooked and coconut milk together.
8. Take them into a large bowl after mixing.
9. Mix them well and then bake your cake.
10. Your cake is ready to be served.

5.9 Thai Banana Spring Rolls Recipe

Preparation Time: 10 minutes

Cooking Time: 10 minutes

Serving: 2

Ingredients:

- Chopped bananas, five
- Shredded coconut, half cup
- Wonton wraps, as required
- Chinese five spice, as needed
- Cooking oil, as required

Instructions:

1. In a large bowl, mix all the ingredients together.
2. Add the mixture into the wonton wrappers.
3. Wrap your rolls.
4. Fry your rolls until they turn golden brown.
5. Dish out and drizzle any sauce if you want on top.
6. Your dish is ready to be served.

5.10 Thai Mango Cake Recipe

Preparation Time: 30 minutes

Cooking Time: 10 minutes

Serving: 4

Ingredients:

- Mangoes, three
- Salt, two tablespoon
- White sugar, two cups
- Cornstarch, one tablespoon
- Water, two cups
- Coconut milk, one cup
- Rice flour, one cup
- Raspberries, aa required

Instructions:

1. Take the mangoes into a bowl.
2. Slice them into small pieces.
3. Add salt to it for taste as required.
4. Take water in a pot and heat it.
5. Take a large bowl and add the sweet rice into it.
6. Cook the rice and add some of the sugar into it for taste.
7. Take another bowl and add coconut milk into it.
8. Mix the palm sugar into the coconut milk.
9. Then mix the sliced mangoes and coconut milk together.

10. Take them into a large bowl after mixing.

11. Add the coconut juice and raspberries into it.

12. Mix them well.

13. Then bake them for fifteen minutes.

14. After cooking, you can refrigerate the cake.

15. Your cake is ready to be served.

5.11 Thai Coconut Cake Recipe

Preparation Time: 10 minutes

Cooking Time: 10 minutes

Serving: 4

Ingredients:

- Coconut, two
- Salt, two tablespoon
- White sugar, two cups
- Cornstarch, one tablespoon
- Water, two cups
- Coconut milk, one cup
- Rice flour, one cup
- Raspberries, aa required

Instructions:

1. Take the coconut juice into a bowl.
2. Add salt to it for taste as required.
3. Take water in a pot and heat it.
4. Take a large bowl and add the sweet rice into it.
5. Cook the rice and add some of sugar into it for taste.

6. Take another bowl and add coconut milk into it.

7. Mix the palm sugar into the coconut milk.

8. Then mix the rice cooked and coconut milk together.

9. Take them into a large bowl after mixing.

10. Add the coconut juice and raspberries into it.

11. Mix them well.

12. Then bake them for fifteen minutes.

13. After cooking you can refrigerate the cake.

14. Your cake is ready to be served.

5.12 Thai Mango Ice Cream Recipe

Preparation Time: 10 minutes

Cooking Time: 15 minutes

Serving: 2

- Mangoes, two
- Coconut milk, half cup
- White sugar, half cup
- Salt, one teaspoon
- Eggs, two
- Lemon extract, one teaspoon
- Almond extract, one teaspoon
- All-purpose flour, two cups

- Butter, one cup

Instructions:
1. Slice the mangoes into small pieces.
2. Take a medium bowl and add the tapioca flour in it.
3. Add one cup of coconut milk and mix well.
4. Then refrigerate it.
5. Take a large bowl and add the spices into it.
6. Add the sugar, the salt and the spices.
7. Mix them well.
8. Mix the warm milk mixture with the flour and the sliced mangoes.
9. Add the eggs, the lemon extract and the almond extract together.
10. Add the baking soda in the mixture.
11. Simmer it for few minutes.
12. Check the thickness of the ice cream.
13. Refrigerate it.
14. Your dish is ready to be served.

5.13 Thai Sticky Black Rice Pudding Recipe

Preparation Time: 15 minutes

Cooking Time: 25 minutes

Serving: 3

Ingredients:

- Black rice, two cups
- Chinese sweet spices, to taste
- Coconut milk, half cup
- White sugar, half cup
- Salt, one teaspoon
- Eggs, two
- Lemon extract, one teaspoon
- Almond extract, one teaspoon
- All-purpose flour, two cups
- Butter, one cup

Instructions:

1. Cook the black rice in the rice cooking pan.
2. Take a medium bowl and add the tapioca flour in it.
3. Add one cup of coconut milk and mix well.
4. Then refrigerate it.
5. Take a large bowl and add the spices into it.
6. Add the sugar, the salt and the spices.
7. Mix them well.
8. Mix the warm milk mixture with the flour and the cooked rice.
9. Add the eggs, lemon extract and almond extract together.

10. Add the baking soda in the mixture.

11. Simmer it for few minutes.

12. Your dish is ready to be served.

5.14 Thai Egg and Coconut Custard Recipe

Preparation Time: 30 minutes

Cooking Time: 10 minutes

Serving: 4

Ingredients:
- Eggs, two
- Coconut, two
- Chinese sweet spices, to taste
- Coconut milk, half cup
- White sugar, half cup
- Salt, one teaspoon
- Lemon extract, one teaspoon
- Almond extract, one teaspoon
- All-purpose flour, two cups
- Butter, one cup

Instructions:
1. Take a medium bowl and add the eggs and the tapioca flour in it.
2. Add one cup of coconut milk and mix well.

3. Then refrigerate it.

4. Take a large bowl and add the spices into it.

5. Add the sugar, the salt and the beaten eggs.

6. Mix them well.

7. Mix the warm milk mixture with the flour and coconut.

8. Add the eggs, lemon extract and almond extract together.

9. Add the baking soda in the mixture.

10. Simmer it for few minutes.

11. Check the thickness of the custard.

12. Your dish is ready to be served.

5.15 Thai Sweet Corn Pudding Recipe

Preparation Time: 10 minutes

Cooking Time: 30 minutes

Serving: 4

Ingredients:

- Butter, one cup
- Sweet corn, one cup
- Eggs, two
- Cherries, two
- All-purpose flour, two cups
- Water, as required

- Baking soda, one tablespoon
- Salt, a pinch
- Walnuts, one cup

Instructions:

1. Take a large bowl and clean it well.
2. Add the sweet corn and the baking soda.
3. Add the salt and the cream.
4. Mix all the ingredients well.
5. Add beaten eggs into the mixture.
6. Pour into the dish and spread evenly.
7. Take a small bowl and add the sugar and the butter.
8. Mix them until it becomes smooth.
9. Add the mixture into flour and mix well.
10. Simmer it for about twenty-five minutes
11. Your dish is ready to be served.

Chapter 6: The World of Traditional Thai Recipes Eaten Only by Thai People

Following are some classic traditional Thai recipes eaten only by Thai people that are rich in healthy nutrients and you can easily make them with the detailed instructions list given in each recipe:

6.1 Patonga (Thai Breakfast Donut) Recipe

Preparation Time: 15 minutes

Cooking Time: 30 minutes

Serving: 3

Ingredients:

- All-purpose flour, one cup
- Baking soda, one cup
- Sugar, two tablespoon
- Water, half cup
- Vegetable oil, two cups
- Milk, two cups
- Walnuts, one cup
- Eggs, four
- Cherries, one cup
- Butter as needed

Instructions:

1. Take a large bowl and clean it well.
2. Add the sugar and the baking soda.
3. Add the salt and the cream.
4. Mix all the ingredients well.
5. Add beaten eggs into the mixture.
6. Pour into the dish and spread evenly.
7. Take a small bowl and add the sugar and the butter.
8. Mix them until become smooth.
9. Add the mixture into flour and mix well.
10. Bake it for about twenty-five minutes.
11. Your dish is ready to be served.

6.2 Khanom Kharuk (Thai Mini Pancakes) Recipe

Preparation Time: 30 minutes

Cooking Time: 50 minutes

Serving: 5

Ingredients:

- Blackberry jam, one cup
- Butter, one cup
- Eggs, two
- Cherries, two

- All-purpose flour, two cups
- Water, as required
- Baking soda, one tablespoon
- Salt, a pinch
- Walnuts, one cup

Instructions:

1. Take a large bowl and clean it well.
2. Add the sugar and the baking soda.
3. Add the salt and the cream.
4. Mix all the ingredients well.
5. Add beaten eggs into the mixture.
6. Add blackberry jam into it.
7. Pour into the dish and spread evenly.
8. Take a small bowl and add the sugar and the butter.
9. Mix them until the mixture becomes smooth.
10. Add the mixture into flour and mix well.
11. Bake it for about thirty-five minutes.
12. Your dish is ready to be served.

6.3 Jauk (The Rice Porridge) Recipe

Preparation Time: 20 minutes
Cooking Time: 20 minutes

Serving: 2

Ingredients:

- Fish sauce, three teaspoon
- Brown cooked rice, two cups
- Ground pork, one cup
- Cilantro, one tablespoon
- Black pepper, to taste
- Chicken broth, four cups
- Egg white, half cup
- Galangal, one slice
- Ginger, two tablespoon
- Palm sugar, one tablespoon
- Lime juice, one tablespoon
- Alfa one rice bran oil, teaspoon
- Coconut milk, one cup
- Bean sprouts, one cup
- Fried shallots, to serve
- Red chili, to serve

Instructions:

1. Cook the rice in rice cooker.
2. Then refrigerate it.
3. Prepare meat balls by mixing all the ingredients one by one
4. Cook it for one minute with continuous stirring.

5. Add the coconut milk into the mixture.

6. Boil the coconut milk along with mixture.

7. Continue boiling for five minutes until water reduces to minimum level.

8. Add the egg whites and mix well.

9. Then take the chicken broth in a separate large pot.

10. Add the lemon grass and galangal in it.

11. Simmer it for five minutes.

12. Then add them in already cooked brown rice.

13. Adjust taste by adding pepper and salt.

14. Your soup is ready to be served.

15. Serve it with chilies and soy sauce.

6.4 Khao Tom (The Rice Porridge Soup) Recipe

Preparation Time: 10 minutes

Cooking Time: 25 minutes

Serving: 3

Ingredients:

- Fish sauce, three teaspoon
- Brown cooked rice, two cups
- Ground pork, one cup

- Cilantro, one tablespoon
- Black pepper, to taste
- Chicken broth, four cups
- Egg white, half cup
- Galangal, one slice
- Ginger, two tablespoon
- Palm sugar, one tablespoon
- Lime juice, one tablespoon
- Alfa one rice bran oil, teaspoon
- Coconut milk, one cup
- Bean sprouts, one cup
- Fried shallots, to serve
- Red chili, to serve

Instructions:

1. Cook the rice in rice cooker.
2. Then refrigerate it.
3. Prepare meat balls by mixing all the ingredients one by one
4. Cook it for one minute with continuous stirring.
5. Add the coconut milk into the mixture.
6. Boil the coconut milk along with mixture.
7. Continue boiling for five minutes until water reduces to minimum level.
8. Add the egg white and mix well.
9. Then take the chicken broth in separate large pot.

10. Add the lemon grass and galangal in it.

11. Simmer it for five minutes.

12. Then add them in already cooked brown rice.

13. Adjust taste by adding pepper and salt.

14. Your soup is ready to be served.

15. Serve it with chilies and soy sauce.

6.5 Dim Sum (Thai Steamed Buns) Recipe

Preparation Time: 50 minutes

Cooking Time: 30 minutes

Serving: 4

Ingredients:

- Ground pork, half pound
- Thin soy sauce, one tablespoon
- Thai pepper powder, half tablespoon
- Sugar, one tablespoon
- Garlic powder, one tablespoon
- Fresh shallot, half tablespoon
- Milk, one cup
- Vegetable oil, one tablespoon
- All-purpose flour, one cup
- Whole wheat flour, half cup

- Salt, to taste
- Water, to kneed
- Cucumber, one
- Yeast, one cup

Instructions:

1. Take a bowl and add the flour into it.
2. Then add the yeast and sugar into it.
3. Add lukewarm water in it.
4. Set aside for half an hour.
5. In another bowl, take the whole wheat flour.
6. Add the yeast dough in it.
7. Then add the salt and some water in it.
8. Then combine the ingredients to form a soft dough.
9. Kneed it for ten minutes.
10. Meanwhile, chop all the vegetables.
11. Mix them with soy sauce, chili vinegar, sugar and salt.
12. Make round forms of dough with the help of the oil.
13. Then bake your buns for ten minutes.
14. Once the buns are steamed, take them out.
15. You can serve Thai buns with salad.

6.6 Thai Sweet Rice Cakes Recipe

Preparation Time: 2 minutes

Cooking Time: 25 minutes

Serving: 2

Ingredients:

- Thai sweet rice, two cups
- Salt, two tablespoon
- White sugar, two cups
- Cornstarch, one tablespoon
- Water, two cups
- Coconut milk, one cup
- Rice flour, one cup
- Pandan essence, as needed
- Raspberries, aa required

Instructions:
1. Take a blender and blend the pandan leaves.
2. Then add the paste type material into a bowl.
3. Press the paste so that all juice comes out.
4. Take the juice and discard the solids.
5. Take water in a pot and heat it.
6. Take a large bowl and add the sweet rice into it.

7. Cook the rice and add some of the sugar into it for taste.

8. Take another bowl and add coconut milk into it.

9. Mix the palm sugar into the coconut milk.

10. Then mix the cooked rice and coconut milk together.

11. Take them into a large bowl after mixing.

12. Add pandan juice and raspberries into it.

13. Mix them well.

14. Then bake them well.

15. After cooking you can refrigerate the cake.

16. Your cake is ready to be served.

6.7 Thai Steamed Pandan Cakes Recipe

Preparation Time: 15 minutes

Cooking Time: 35 minutes

Serving: 2

Ingredients:

- Pandan leaves, one bunch
- Tapioca starch, one cup
- Arrowroot starch, one cup
- Water, two cups
- Coconut milk, one cup

- Rice flour, one cup
- Jasmine tea, one cup

Instructions:

1. Take a blender and blend the pandan leaves.
2. Then add the paste type material into a bowl.
3. Press the paste so that all juice comes out.
4. Take the juice and discard the solids.
5. Take water in a pot and heat it.
6. Take a large bowl and add rice flour into it.
7. Then whisk it with tapioca starch and arrowroot starch.
8. Take another bowl and add coconut milk into it.
9. Mix the palm sugar into the coconut milk.
10. Then mix the rice flour and coconut milk together.
11. Take them into a large bowl after mixing.
12. Add pandan juice and jasmine tea into it.
13. Mix them well and cook them efficiently.
14. After cooking you can refrigerate the whole food.
15. Your cake is ready to be served.

6.8 Thai Carrot and Radish Salad Recipe

Preparation Time: 5 minutes

Cooking Time: 5 minutes

Serving: 3

Ingredients:

- Carrots, two
- Radishes, ten
- Spring onions, three
- Gem lettuce, separated into leaves
- Lime zest, one
- Chili sauce, one teaspoon
- Fish sauce, one tablespoon
- Rice vinegar, one tablespoon
- Sugar, one tablespoon
- Sesame oil, one tablespoon
- Sesame seeds, one cup

Instructions:

1. Take a large bowl to put all the ingredients into it.
2. First of all, slice the carrots into small pieces so that proper mixing can be done.

3. Then slice the radish in the same way.

4. Put them into the bowl.

5. Add chili sauce and fish sauce into the bowl.

6. Add all spices one by one.

7. Add the rice vinegar in such a way that equal distribution can be done.

8. Take the gem lettuce in a separate bowl.

9. Add the lime zest and juice into it.

10.   Add the spring onions, sesame seeds and sesame oil into it.

11.   Mix all the ingredients so that a good paste is formed

12.   Then add it in the first bowl with carrots and radishes.

13.   You can add sugar as per your requirement.

14.   Your salad is ready to be served with chili sauce.

6.9 Thai Fish Broth with Vegetables Recipe

Preparation Time: 10 minutes

Cooking Time: 25 minutes

Serving: 4

Ingredients:

- Brown rice noodles, one cup
- Chicken, two cups

- Red curry paste, one teaspoon
- Fish sauce, one tablespoon
- White fish, one bowl
- Red chili, to serve
- Prawns, one cup
- Fried shallots, to serve
- Salt, to taste
- Pepper, to taste
- Lime leaves, one cup

Instructions:

1. Take a large saucepan and add oil in it.
2. Heat it over medium high heat.
3. Add the brown rice noodles into it.
4. Cook it for one minute with the continuous stirring.
5. Add the chicken into the mixture.
6. Boil the chicken and curry paste along with mixture.
7. Continue boiling for five minutes until water reduces to minimum level.
8. Add the lime leaves in a separate bowl.
9. And cover it with the boiling water for five minutes.
10. Add fish into the mixture and boil until the meat becomes soft and tender.

11.   Add the fish sauce, lime juice and peas into the mixture.

12.   Add the prawns to the mixture in the end having all the ingredients.

13.   Cook for five minutes so that color and texture of the fish become suitable.

14.   Your dish is ready to be served with the sauces and spices you want.

6.10 Thai Prawn and Coconut Soup Recipe

Preparation Time: 10 minutes

Cooking Time: 25 minutes

Serving: 2

Ingredients:

- sauce, three teaspoon
- Palm sugar, one tablespoon
- Lime juice, one tablespoon
- Peas, trimmed, one cup
- Peeled prawns, two cups
- Alfa one rice bran oil, teaspoon
- Coconut milk, one cup
- Bean sprouts, one cup
- Fried shallots, to serve

- Red chili, to serve
- Red curry paste, half cup
- Noodles, one packet

Instructions:

1. Take a large saucepan and add oil in it.
2. Heat it over medium high heat.
3. Add curry paste into it.
4. Cook it for one minute with continuous stirring.
5. Add the coconut milk into the mixture.
6. Boil the coconut milk along with mixture.
7. Continue boiling for five minutes until water reduces to minimum level.
8. Add the noodles in a separate bowl.
9. Cover it with the boiling water for five minutes.
10. Then remove the noodles with the help of fork and drain it.
11. Add the fish sauce, lime juice and peas into the mixture.
12. Add the prawns to the soup.
13. Cook for five minutes.
14. Your soup is ready to be served.

Conclusion

While living a busy life, food becomes the one of the source of happiness for individuals in the 21st century. Different cuisines are available in the world and each of them being totally different from the other, adds delight to the people's lives. Thai cuisine covers dishes from Thailand and Thai foods which are extremely popular in the whole world.

In this book, we have discussed different aspects of Thai cuisine and not only the recipes. We discussed in detail the history and origin of Thai foods. The various spices used in Thai cooking have enormous amount of amazing properties that has such positive and healthy impact on our overall health. This cookbook includes 70 recipes that consist of breakfast, lunch, dinner, dessert, and the recipes that are only eaten by Thai people. You can easily make these recipes at home without supervision of any kind. So start cooking today and enjoy the Thai cuisine more than ever.

VEGETARIAN

THAI

COOKBOOK

70 Recipes for Asian Foods from Thailand

By

Maki Blanc

The trademarks that are used are without any consent, and the publication of the trademark is without permission or backing by the trademark owner. All trademarks and brands within this book are for clarifying purposes only and are owned by the owners themselves, not affiliated with this document.

Introduction

Thai food culture is very famous for its stunning food choices and amazing taste. The good contains sweet, spicy, sour and salty taste in a single bite. Food is loved a lot and the Thai people are huge fans of healthy and nutritious food.

Vegetarian foods are eaten all across the globe. People usually adopt the vegetarian diet for religious or personal reasons. Some People usually think that vegetarian foods may not taste as good as non-vegetarian foods but the vegetarian Thai food would change your perspective related to this thought.

From cooked vegetable sautés to hand beaten servings of mixed greens, you will be in heaven if you love cooking as well as eating with the assortment and proportion of food in the Thai cooking style given in this book. You will get in excess of 70 assorted vegetarian recipes. The recipes include vegetarian breakfast recipes, vegetarian lunch recipes, vegetarian dinner recipes, vegetarian dessert recipes, and vegetarian snack recipes that you can without a doubt start cooking at home with the definite instructions present underneath each recipe plan.

Setting up your simple Thai food at home without the need to arrange food from some eateries can turn out to be exceptionally simple once you begin perusing this book. Anyway, why sit tight and wait? Allow yourself to dive into the universe of Thai food.

Chapter 1: The World of Vegetarian Thai Breakfast Recipes

You have saved time, cash and calories by skipping your favorite Thai cafés and cooking by yourself at home. In this chapter you will learn some amazing Thai vegetarian breakfast dishes that you can easily make at home on your own.

1.1 Pak Boong Recipe

Preparation Time: 20 minutes

Cooking Time: 20 minutes

Serving: 4

Ingredients:

- Oyster sauce, one tablespoon
- Fresh Thai chili peppers, two
- Korean soybean paste, one tablespoon
- Sugar, half tablespoon
- Mirim, one tablespoon
- Soy sauce, half tablespoon
- Minced garlic, two teaspoon
- Cooking oil, three tablespoon
- Morning glory, two cups
- Salt, as required

- Chopped fresh cilantro, as required

Instructions:

1. Take a large pan.
2. Add the cooking oil into the pan and heat it.
3. Add the morning glory into the pan and stir-fry it.
4. Add the minced garlic along with the morning glory.
5. Cook your ingredients for five minutes until the color of the morning glory changes.
6. Add the soy sauce, mirim, sugar, fresh Thai chili peppers, Korean soy bean paste and oyster sauce into the mixture.
7. Cook your dish for ten minutes.
8. Dish out your pak boong and garnish it with chopped fresh cilantro leaves.
9. Your dish is ready to be served.

1.2 Thai Vegetarian Omelet Recipe

Preparation Time: 30 minutes

Cooking Time: 10 minutes

Serving: 4

Ingredients:

- Mushrooms, two
- Onions, half cup
- Rice wine, one tablespoon
- Black pepper, to taste
- Salt, to taste
- Starch, a quarter teaspoon
- Kohlrabi, one cup
- Ginger, one slice
- Soy sauce, one tablespoon
- Oil, one tablespoon
- Cilantro, as required

Instructions:

13.   Beat the eggs with water, black pepper and salt.

14.   Add oil to a wok, and then add the beaten eggs.

15.   Sprinkle the vegetables on top.

16.   Add the rest of the ingredients on top of your egg mixture.

17.   Fold the egg and then cook it on both sides.

18.	When the eggs are done, dish them out.

19.	Add on top of the eggs the chopped cilantro leaves.

20.	Your dish is ready to be served.

1.3 Thai Rice Congee Recipe

Preparation Time: 20 minutes

Cooking Time: 20 minutes

Serving: 2

Ingredients:

- Rice, one cup
- Cream, two tablespoon
- Butter, one cup
- Eggs, two
- Cherries, two
- All-purpose flour, two cups
- Water, as required
- Baking soda, one tablespoon
- Salt, a pinch
- Pepper, to taste

Instructions:

1. Take a large pan and clean it well.

2. Add the sugar and the baking soda and the rice into it.

3. Add the salt and the cream.

4. Add all-purpose flour into it so that congee can be smooth.

5. Add the crushed walnuts into the mixture.

6. Mix all the ingredients well.

7. Add beaten eggs into the mixture.

8. Pour into the dish and spread evenly.

9. Take a small bowl and add the butter.

10. Mix them until the mixture becomes smooth and then add it into your dish.

11. Add the salt as required.

12. Simmer it for about five minutes.

13. Your dish is ready to be served with cherries and the walnuts.

14. You can refrigerate your dish as well.

1.4 Thai Tofu Omelet Recipe

Preparation Time: 30 minutes

Cooking Time: 10 minutes

Serving: 4

Ingredients:
- Chopped tofu, one cup
- Red chili paste, two tablespoon

- Mushrooms, two
- Onions, half cup
- Eggs, four
- Rice wine, one tablespoon
- Black pepper, to taste
- Salt, to taste
- Green chilies, a quarter teaspoon
- Ginger, one slice
- Soy sauce, one tablespoon
- Oil, one tablespoon
- Cilantro, as required

Instructions:

1. Beat the eggs with the red wine, black pepper and salt.
2. Add oil to a large pan, and then add the beaten eggs.
3. Sprinkle the vegetables on top.
4. Add the chopped tofu on top of your mixture.
5. Add the rest of the ingredients on top of your egg mixture.
6. Fold the egg and then cook it on both sides.
7. When the eggs are done, dish them out.
8. Add on top of the eggs the chopped cilantro leaves.
9. Your dish is ready to be served.

1.5 Thai Black Rice Porridge Recipe

Preparation Time: 20 minutes

Cooking Time: 20 minutes

Serving: 2

Ingredients:

- Fish sauce, three teaspoon
- Cooked black rice, two cups
- Vegetable broth, one cup
- Cilantro, one tablespoon
- Black pepper, to taste
- Egg white, half cup
- Galangal, one slice
- Ginger, two tablespoon
- Palm sugar, one tablespoon
- Lime juice, one tablespoon
- Alfa one rice bran oil, teaspoon
- Coconut milk, one cup
- Bean sprouts, one cup
- Fried shallots, to serve
- Red chili, to serve

Instructions:

16.   Cook the black rice in rice cooker.

17.   Add the coconut milk into the mixture.

18.   Boil the coconut milk along with mixture.

19.   Continue boiling for five minutes until water reduces to minimum level.

20.   Add the egg white and mix well.

21.   Then take the vegetable broth in separate large pot.

22.   Add the lemon grass and galangal in it.

23.   Simmer it for five minutes.

24.   Then add them in already cooked black rice.

25.   Adjust taste by adding pepper and salt.

26.   Your porridge is ready to be served.

27.   Serve it with chilies and soy sauce.

1.6 Vegetarian Thai Egg and Chili Recipe

Preparation Time: 30 minutes

Cooking Time: 10 minutes

Serving: 4

Ingredients:
- Sugar, two teaspoon
- Fresh Thai chilies, four
- Eggs, four
- White pepper, a quarter teaspoon
- Water, half cup

- Scallions, one
- Sesame oil, two teaspoon
- Vegetable oil, three tablespoon

Instructions:

1. Heat the wok and add the oil.
2. Add the eggs and mix them.
3. Remove the scrambled eggs into a dish.
4. Add one more tablespoon of oil to the wok, and add the Thai chilies and scallions.
5. Stir-fry for one minute, and then add two teaspoons sugar, half teaspoon salt, and a quarter cup water.
6. Add the cooked eggs in the mixture.
7. Your dish is ready to be served.

1.7 Spicy Thai Kale and Coconut Fried Rice Recipe

Preparation Time: 30 minutes

Cooking Time: 10 minutes

Serving: 4

Ingredients:

- Sliced kale, one cup
- Shredded unsweetened coconut, half cup
- Red chilies, two
- Coconut milk, one cup
- Sliced green onions, half cup
- White peppercorns, one teaspoon
- Cilantro, one cup
- Fresh ginger, one teaspoon
- Fish sauce, one tablespoon
- Soy sauce, one tablespoon
- Chili garlic sauce, two tablespoon
- Fresh cilantro leaves, half cup
- Fresh basil leaves, a quarter cup
- Vegetable broth, one can
- Minced lemon grass, one teaspoon
- Egg, one large
- Cooked rice, as required
-

Instructions:

12. Add all the ingredients of the curry into a wok.

13.   Add the vegetable broth and sauces into the mixture.

14.   Cook your dish for ten minutes.

15.   Add the cooked rice into the mixture.

16.   Mix the rice well and cook it for five minutes.

17.   Add the egg into the wok by pushing the rest of the ingredients to a side.

18.   Cook the egg and then mix the rest of the ingredients into it.

19.   Add the sliced kale and shredded coconut.

20.   Cook your dish for five more minutes.

21.   Add the cilantro into the dish.

22.   Mix your rice and then dish it out.

23.   Your dish is ready to be served.

1.8 Vegetarian Thai Coconut Milk Rice Porridge Recipe

Preparation Time: 20 minutes

Cooking Time: 20 minutes

Serving: 2

Ingredients:

- Fish sauce, three teaspoon
- Cooked white rice, two cups
- Cilantro, one tablespoon
- Black pepper, to taste
- Egg whites, half cup
- Galangal, one slice
- Ginger, two tablespoon
- Palm sugar, one tablespoon
- Lime juice, one tablespoon
- Alfa one rice bran oil, teaspoon
- Coconut milk, two cup
- Fried shallots, to serve
- Red chili, to serve

Instructions:

1. Cook the white rice in rice cooker.
2. Add the coconut milk into the mixture.
3. Boil the coconut milk along with mixture.
4. Continue boiling for five minutes until water reduces to minimum level.
5. Add the egg whites and mix well.
6. Add the lemon grass and galangal in it.
7. Simmer it for five minutes.

8. Then add them in already cooked white rice.

9. Adjust taste by adding pepper and salt.

10.   Your porridge is ready to be served.

11.   Serve it with chilies and soy sauce.

1.9 Vegetarian Thai Omelet Soup Recipe

Preparation Time: 30 minutes

Cooking Time: 10 minutes

Serving: 4

Ingredients:
- Mushrooms, two
- Onions, half cup
- Rice wine, one tablespoon
- Black pepper, to taste
- Salt, to taste
- Starch, a quarter teaspoon
- Kohlrabi, one cup
- Ginger, one slice
- Soy sauce, one tablespoon
- Oil, one tablespoon
- Cilantro, as required

For soup:
- Vegetable stock, four cups
- Thai basil, half cup

- Salt, to taste
- Black pepper, to taste
- Lime juice, one tablespoon
- Thai red pepper, half teaspoon

Instructions:

1. Beat the eggs with water, black pepper and salt.
2. Add oil to a wok, and then add the beaten eggs.
3. Sprinkle the vegetables on top.
4. Add the rest of the ingredients on top of your egg mixture.
5. Fold the egg and then cook it on both sides.
6. When the eggs are done, dish them out.
7. In the wok, add the vegetable stock and the spices for the soup.
8. When the soup boils enough, add the omelet into the soup.
9. Cook your soup for five minutes.
10. Garnish your soup with the chopped cilantro leaves.
11. Your dish is ready to be served.

1.10 Thai Scrambled Tofu and Egg Recipe

Preparation Time: 30 minutes

Cooking Time: 10 minutes

Serving: 4

Ingredients:

- Butter, two tablespoon
- Coconut cream, half cup
- Chopped tofu, half pound
- Salt, to taste
- Southwest chili sauce, two tablespoon
- Black pepper, to taste
- Chopped fresh chives, as required
- Eggs, twelve
- Onions, one
- Chopped garlic, one teaspoon

Instructions:

1. In a large wok, add the butter and let it meltdown.
2. Add in the chopped onion.
3. Cook the onions until soft.
4. Add in the garlic.
5. Mix the onions and garlic for two minutes and add in the chopped tofu pieces.
6. Add the eggs and let it cook.
7. Scramble the mixture.
8. Add in the salt and pepper.
9. Add in the coconut cream in the end.
10. When the eggs are done, dish them out.
11. Add the fresh chopped chives on top.

12.   Your dish is ready to be served.

1.11 Vegetarian Thai Rice Soup Recipe

Preparation Time: 30 minutes

Cooking Time: 10 minutes

Serving: 4

Ingredients:

- White peppercorns, one teaspoon
- Cilantro, one cup
- Ginger paste, two tablespoon
- Fish sauce, one tablespoon
- Soy sauce, one and a half tablespoon
- Vegetable stock, three cup
- Jasmine rice, four cups
- Garlic cloves, four

Instructions:

11.   Crush the white peppercorns until they turn into powdered form.

12.   At that point add garlic and cilantro and pound until they are crushed.

13.   Season with fish sauce and soy sauce, at that point taste and add more if you prefer.

14. When prepared to serve, heat the stock to the point of boiling.

15. Add the rice into the stock.

16. Add the soup into a bowl.

17. Garnish it with cilantro leaves.

18. Your dish is ready to be served.

1.12 Vegetarian Thai Fried Rice Recipe

Preparation Time: 30 minutes

Cooking Time: 10 minutes

Serving: 4

Ingredients:
- Thai chilies, two
- Sliced green onions, half cup
- White peppercorns, one teaspoon
- Cilantro, one cup
- Fresh ginger, one teaspoon

- Fish sauce, one tablespoon
- Soy sauce, one tablespoon
- Chili garlic sauce, two tablespoon
- Fresh cilantro leaves, half cup
- Thai basil leaves, a quarter cup
- Mixed vegetables, one cup
- Cooked rice, as required

Instructions:

1. Heat a large pan.
2. Add the vegetable broth and sauces into the mixture.
3. Cook your dish for ten minutes.
4. Add the cooked rice into the mixture.
5. Mix the rice well and cook it for five minutes.
6. Add the mixed vegetable and rest of the ingredients into the mixture.
7. Cook your dish for five more minutes.
8. Add the cilantro into the dish.
9. Mix your rice and then dish it out.
10. Your dish is ready to be served.

Chapter 2: The World of Vegetarian Thai Lunch Recipes

Thai lunch recipes consist of amazing dishes that are healthy, nutritious and flavorful at the same time. Following are some amazing Thai lunch recipes that you can easily make at home:

2.1 Vegetarian Thai Coconut Soup Recipe

Preparation Time: 30 minutes

Cooking Time: 10 minutes

Serving: 4

Ingredients:

- Water, two cups
- Galangal, one can
- Minced garlic, one teaspoon
- Minced ginger, one teaspoon
- Chopped onion, half cup
- Minced ginger, half tablespoon
- Lemon grass, two sticks
- Fish sauce, two tablespoon
- Shredded coconut, one cup
- Coconut milk, one cup

- Cilantro, a quarter cup
- Olive oil, one tablespoon

Instructions:

11.   Take a large sauce wok.

12.   Add the chopped onion and olive oil.

13.   Cook your chopped onion.

14.   When the onions are cooked then add the galangal, garlic and ginger.

15.   Add the coconut milk.

16.   Cook your ingredients until they start boiling.

17.   Add in the shredded coconut, lemon grass and rest of the ingredients into your soup.

18.   Cook your ingredients for ten minutes.

19.   Garnish it with cilantro leaves.

20.   Your dish is ready to be served.

2.2 Vegetarian Thai Tomato Soup Recipe

Preparation Time: 30 minutes

Cooking Time: 10 minutes

Serving: 4

Ingredients:

- Galangal, one can

- Vegetable stock, two cups
- Minced garlic, one teaspoon
- Palm sugar, two tablespoon
- Shallot, one
- Kaffir lime leaves, four
- Lime wedges
- Chopped tomatoes, one cup
- Lemon grass, two sticks
- Fish sauce, two tablespoon
- Tomato puree, one cup
- Coconut milk, one cup
- Cilantro, a quarter cup
- Olive oil, one tablespoon

Instructions:

12. Take a large sauce pan.

13. Add the shallots and olive oil.

14. Add the galangal, vegetable stock, and minced garlic.

15. Cook your ingredients until they start boiling.

16. Add in the tomatoes, tomato puree, lemon grass and rest of the ingredients into your soup.

17. Cook your ingredients for ten minutes.

18. Garnish it with cilantro leaves.

19. Your dish is ready to be served.

2.3 Vegetarian Thai Creamy Red Lentil Curry Recipe

Preparation Time: 30 minutes

Cooking Time: 10 minutes

Serving: 4

Ingredients:

- Vegetable stock, two cups
- Minced garlic, one teaspoon
- Palm sugar, two tablespoon
- Coconut cream, one cup
- Shallot, one
- Kaffir lime leaves, four
- Lime wedges
- Lemon grass, two sticks
- Fish sauce, two tablespoon
- Coconut milk, one cup
- Cilantro, a quarter cup
- Red lentils, half pound
- Olive oil, one tablespoon

Instructions:

12.   Take a large sauce pan.

13.   Add the shallots and olive oil.

14.   Cook your shallots and then add the red lentil.

15.   When the red lentil is half cooked, add the vegetable stock, and minced garlic.

16.   Add the palm sugar and coconut milk.

17.   Cook your ingredients until they start boiling.

18.   Add in the coconut cream and rest of the ingredients into your soup.

19.   Cook your ingredients for ten minutes.

20.   Garnish it with cilantro leaves.

21.   Your dish is ready to be served.

2.4 Vegetarian Thai Chili Lime Noodles Recipe

Preparation Time: 30 minutes

Cooking Time: 10 minutes

Serving: 4

Ingredients:
- Mixed vegetables, two cups
- Sliced green onions, half cup
- White peppercorns, one teaspoon
- Cilantro, one cup

- Fresh ginger, one teaspoon
- Fish sauce, one tablespoon
- Soy sauce, one tablespoon
- Chili lime sauce, one cup
- Chili garlic sauce, two tablespoon
- Fresh cilantro leaves, half cup
- Fresh basil leaves, a quarter cup
- Vegetable broth, one cup
- Noodles, as required

Instructions:

9. Add all the ingredients of the sauce into a wok.

10. Add the chili lime sauce, mixed vegetables, vegetable broth and sauces into the mixture.

11. Cook your dish for ten minutes.

12. Add the noodles into the mixture once the sauce is ready.

13. Mix the noodles well and cook them for five minutes.

14. Add the cilantro into the dish.

15. Cook your noodles and then dish them out.

16. Your dish is ready to be served.

2.5 Vegetarian Thai Garlic and Broccoli Stir-Fry Recipe

Preparation Time: 10 minutes

Cooking Time: 20 minutes

Serving: 4

Ingredients:

- Fish sauce, two tablespoon
- Soy sauce, half cup
- Tomatoes, two
- Broccoli florets, two cups
- Cilantro, half cup
- Salt and pepper, to taste
- Minced ginger, half tablespoon
- Vegetable oil, two tablespoon
- Red chili peppers, three
- Onion, one
- Toasted nuts, half cups
- Scallions, half cup
- Minced garlic, one teaspoon

Instructions:

1. In a large wok, add the shallots and oil.

2. Cook your shallots and then add the ginger and garlic.

3. Cook your ginger and garlic.

4. Add the broccoli florets and the rest of the ingredients into your dish except the toasted nuts.

5. Cook your dish for five minutes.

6. Garnish your dish with cilantro.

7. Your dish is ready to be served.

2.6 Vegetarian Thai Cauliflower Curry Recipe

Preparation Time: 30 minutes

Cooking Time: 10 minutes

Serving: 4

Ingredients:

- Vegetable stock, two cups
- Minced garlic, one teaspoon
- Thai spices, two tablespoon
- Shallot, one
- Kaffir lime leaves, four
- Lime wedges
- Lemon grass, two sticks
- Fish sauce, two tablespoon
- Coconut milk, one cup

- Cilantro, a quarter cup
- Cauliflower florets, half pound
- Olive oil, one tablespoon

Instructions:

1. Take a large sauce pan.
2. Add the shallots and olive oil.
3. Cook your shallots and then add the cauliflower florets.
4. When the cauliflower florets are half cooked, add the vegetable stock, and minced garlic.
5. Add the coconut milk.
6. Cook your ingredients for ten minutes.
7. Garnish it with cilantro leaves.
8. Your dish is ready to be served.

2.7 Vegetarian Thai Quinoa Recipe

Preparation Time: 30 minutes

Cooking Time: 25 minutes

Serving: 4

Ingredients:

- Minced garlic, two tablespoon
- Minced ginger, two tablespoon
- Cilantro, half cup
- Olive oil, two tablespoon
- Chopped tomatoes, one cup
- Quinoa, one cup
- Turmeric powder, one teaspoon
- Onion, one cup
- Vegetable broth, one cup
- Smoked paprika, half teaspoon
- Water, one cup

Instructions:

1. Take a pan.
2. Add in the oil and onions.
3. Cook the onions until they become soft and fragrant.
4. Add in the chopped garlic and ginger.
5. Cook the mixture and add the tomatoes into it.
6. Add the spices.

7. When the tomatoes are done, add the quinoa into it.

8. Add in the broth.

9. Mix the ingredients carefully and cover your pan.

10. When your quinoa is done, add in the cilantro.

11. Mix the quinoa and let it cook for an additional five minutes.

12. Your dish is ready to be served.

2.8 Vegetarian Thai Red Butternut Squash Curry Recipe

Preparation Time: 30 minutes

Cooking Time: 10 minutes

Serving: 4

Ingredients:

- Thai red curry paste, one tablespoon
- Vegetable stock, two cups
- Minced garlic, one teaspoon
- Thai spices, two tablespoon
- Shallot, one
- Kaffir lime leaves, four
- Lime wedges
- Lemon grass, two sticks

- Fish sauce, two tablespoon
- Coconut milk, one cup
- Cilantro, a quarter cup
- Butternut squash pieces, half pound
- Olive oil, one tablespoon

Instructions:

1. Take a large sauce pan.
2. Add the shallots and olive oil.
3. Cook your shallots and then add the butternut squash pieces.
4. When the butternut squash pieces are half cooked, add the galangal, vegetable stock, and minced garlic.
5. Add the Thai red curry paste into your curry.
6. Add the coconut milk.
7. Cook your ingredients until it starts boiling.
8. Garnish it with cilantro leaves.
9. Your dish is ready to be served.

2.9 Vegetarian Thai Cashew Vegetables Recipe

Preparation Time: 30 minutes

Cooking Time: 10 minutes

Serving: 4

Ingredients:

- Mixed vegetables, two cups
- Sliced green onions, half cup
- White peppercorns, one teaspoon
- Cilantro, one cup
- Fresh ginger, one teaspoon
- Fish sauce, one tablespoon
- Soy sauce, one tablespoon
- Chili garlic sauce, two tablespoon
- Fresh cilantro leaves, half cup
- Fresh basil leaves, a quarter cup
- Vegetable broth, one cup
- Cashew nuts, one cup

Instructions:

1. Add all the ingredients of the sauce into a wok.
2. Add the mixed vegetables, vegetable broth and sauces into the mixture.
3. Cook your dish for ten minutes.
4. Add the cashew nuts into the mixture once the sauce is ready.

5. Mix the cashew nuts well and cook it for five minutes.

6. Add the cilantro into the dish.

7. Cook your cashew nuts and then dish it out.

8. Your dish is ready to be served.

2.10 Vegetarian Thai Vegetable and Potato Yellow Curry Recipe

Preparation Time: 30 minutes

Cooking Time: 10 minutes

Serving: 4

Ingredients:

- Yellow curry paste, two tablespoon
- Vegetable stock, two cups
- Minced garlic, one teaspoon
- Thai spices, two tablespoon
- Shallot, one
- Mixed vegetables, half cup
- Kaffir lime leaves, four
- Lime wedges
- Lemon grass, two sticks
- Fish sauce, two tablespoon
- Coconut milk, one cup
- Cilantro, a quarter cup
- Potatoes, half pound
- Olive oil, one tablespoon

Instructions:

1. Take a large sauce pan.
2. Add the shallots and olive oil.
3. Cook your shallots and then add the vegetables and potatoes.
4. Add the vegetable stock, and minced garlic.
5. Add the coconut milk.
6. Add the yellow curry paste and the rest of the ingredients.
7. Cook your ingredients for ten minutes.
8. Garnish it with cilantro leaves.
9. Your dish is ready to be served.

2.11 Vegetarian Thai Jackfruit and Potato Curry Recipe

Preparation Time: 30 minutes

Cooking Time: 10 minutes

Serving: 4

Ingredients:

- Jackfruit chunks, two cups
- Vegetable stock, two cups
- Minced garlic, one teaspoon
- Thai spices, two tablespoon
- Shallot, one

- Kaffir lime leaves, four
- Lime wedges
- Lemon grass, two sticks
- Fish sauce, two tablespoon
- Coconut milk, one cup
- Cilantro, a quarter cup
- Potatoes, half pound
- Olive oil, one tablespoon

Instructions:

1. Take a large sauce pan.
2. Add the shallots and olive oil.
3. Cook your shallots and then add the potatoes.
4. Add the vegetable stock, and minced garlic.
5. Add the coconut milk.
6. Add the jackfruit chunks and the rest of the ingredients.
7. Cook your ingredients for ten minutes.
8. Garnish it with cilantro leaves.
9. Your dish is ready to be served.

2.12 Vegetarian Thai Sweet Chili Tofu Recipe

Preparation Time: 30 minutes

Cooking Time: 10 minutes

Serving: 4

Ingredients:

- Mixed vegetables, two cups
- Sliced green onions, half cup
- White peppercorns, one teaspoon
- Cilantro, one cup
- Fresh ginger, one teaspoon
- Fish sauce, one tablespoon
- Soy sauce, one tablespoon
- Chili paste, one tablespoon
- Tofu cubes, two cup
- Chili garlic sauce, two tablespoon
- Fresh cilantro leaves, half cup
- Fresh basil leaves, a quarter cup
- Vegetable broth, one cup

Instructions:

1. Add all the ingredients of the sauce into a wok.
2. Add the chili paste, mixed vegetables, vegetable broth and sauces into the mixture.
3. Cook your dish for ten minutes.
4. Add the tofu cubes and the rest of the ingredients into the mixture once the sauce is ready.
5. Mix the tofu cubes well and cook it for five minutes.
6. Add the cilantro into the dish.
7. Your dish is ready to be served.

2.13 Vegetarian Thai Peanut and Chickpea Buddha Bowl Recipe

Preparation Time: 10 minutes

Cooking Time: 20 minutes

Serving: 4

Ingredients:

- Minced ginger, two tablespoon
- Lemon juice, half cup
- Cilantro, one cup
- Olive oil, two tablespoon
- Chopped tomatoes, one cup
- Wild rice, one cup

- Turmeric powder, one teaspoon
- Onion, one cup
- Peanuts, one cup
- Cooked chickpeas, one cup
- Smoked paprika, half teaspoon
- Chopped carrots, one cup
- Minced garlic, two tablespoon

Instructions:

1. Take a pan.
2. Add in the oil and onions.
3. Cook the onions until they become soft and fragrant.
4. Add in the chopped garlic and ginger.
5. Cook the mixture and add the tomatoes into it.
6. Add the spices.
7. When the tomatoes are done, add the chickpeas into it.
8. Mix the ingredients carefully and place your mixture into the oven.
9. When your chickpeas are done, dish them out.
10. In a bowl, place the chickpeas with the peanuts.
11. Add cilantro on top.
12. Your dish is ready to be served.

2.14 Vegetarian Thai Chickpea and Coconut Rice Recipe

Preparation Time: 30 minutes

Cooking Time: 10 minutes

Serving: 4

Ingredients:

- Thai chilies, two
- Sliced green onions, half cup
- White peppercorns, one teaspoon
- Cilantro, one cup
- Fresh ginger, one teaspoon
- Fish sauce, one tablespoon
- Soy sauce, one tablespoon
- Shredded coconut, two tablespoon
- Fresh cilantro leaves, half cup
- Thai basil leaves, a quarter cup
- Cooked chickpeas, one cup
- Cooked rice, as required

Instructions:

1. Heat a large pan.
2. Add the vegetable broth and sauces into the mixture.
3. Cook your dish for ten minutes.

4. Add the cooked rice into the mixture.

5. Mix the rice well and cook it for five minutes.

6. Add the cooked chickpeas and rest of the ingredients into the mixture.

7. Cook your dish for five more minutes.

8. Add the cilantro into the dish.

9. Mix your rice and then dish it out.

10. Your dish is ready to be served.

2.15 Vegetarian Thai Black Pepper Greens and Tofu Curry Recipe

Preparation Time: 30 minutes

Cooking Time: 10 minutes

Serving: 4

Ingredients:
- Vegetable stock, two cups
- Minced garlic, one teaspoon
- Thai spices, two tablespoon
- Shallot, one
- Kaffir lime leaves, four
- Green vegetables, two cups
- Lemon grass, two sticks
- Fish sauce, two tablespoon
- Black pepper, two teaspoon

- Coconut milk, one cup
- Cilantro, a quarter cup
- Tofu cubes, half pound
- Olive oil, one tablespoon

Instructions:
1. Take a large sauce pan.
2. Add the shallots and olive oil.
3. Cook your shallots and then add the greens and tofu cubes.
4. When the ingredients are half cooked, add the vegetable stock, and minced garlic.
5. Add the coconut milk.
6. Add all the rest of the ingredients.
7. Cook your ingredients for ten minutes.
8. Garnish it with cilantro leaves.
9. Your dish is ready to be served.

Chapter 3: The World of Vegetarian Thai Dinner Recipes

This Chapter contains those yummy Thai dinner recipes that you have been longing to make in your kitchen.

3.1 Vegetarian Thai Yellow Tofu Curry Recipe

Preparation Time: 30 minutes

Cooking Time: 10 minutes

Serving: 4

Ingredients:

- Yellow curry paste, two tablespoon
- Vegetable stock, two cups
- Minced garlic, one teaspoon
- Thai spices, two tablespoon
- Shallot, one
- Galangal, half teaspoon
- Mixed vegetables, half cup
- Kaffir lime leaves, four
- Lemon grass, two sticks
- Fish sauce, two tablespoon

- Coconut milk, one cup
- Cilantro, a quarter cup
- Tofu cubes, half pound
- Olive oil, one tablespoon

Instructions:

1. Take a large sauce pan.
2. Add the shallots and olive oil.
3. Cook your shallots and then add the vegetables and tofu cubes.
4. Add the galangal, vegetable stock, and minced garlic.
5. Add the coconut milk.
6. Add the yellow curry paste and the rest of the ingredients.
7. Cook your ingredients for ten minutes.
8. Garnish it with cilantro leaves.
9. Your dish is ready to be served.

3.2 Vegetarian Thai Potato, Spinach and Chickpea Curry Recipe

Preparation Time: 30 minutes

Cooking Time: 10 minutes

Serving: 4

Ingredients:

- Vegetable stock, two cups
- Minced garlic, one teaspoon
- Thai spices, two tablespoon
- Shallot, one
- Kaffir lime leaves, four
- Spinach, two cup
- Lemon grass, two sticks
- Fish sauce, two tablespoon
- Potato cubes, two cups
- Galangal, half teaspoon
- Coconut milk, one cup
- Cilantro, a quarter cup
- Chickpeas, half pound
- Olive oil, one tablespoon

Instructions:

1. Take a large sauce pan.
2. Add the shallots and olive oil.

3. Cook your shallots and then add the chickpeas and potatoes.

4. When the ingredients are half cooked, add the galangal, vegetable stock, and minced garlic.

5. Add the coconut milk.

6. Add the spinach and all the rest of the ingredients.

7. Cook your ingredients for ten minutes.

8. Garnish it with cilantro leaves.

9. Your dish is ready to be served.

3.3 Vegetarian Thai Massaman Curry Recipe

Preparation Time: 30 minutes

Cooking Time: 25 minutes

Serving: 4

Ingredients:

- Minced garlic, two tablespoon
- Minced ginger, two tablespoon
- Cilantro, half cup
- Olive oil, two tablespoon
- Chopped tomatoes, one cup
- Massaman, one cup
- Turmeric powder, one teaspoon
- Onion, one cup

- Vegetable broth, one cup
- Smoked paprika, half teaspoon
- Water, one cup

Instructions:

1. Take a pan.
2. Add in the oil and onions.
3. Cook the onions until they become soft and fragrant.
4. Add in the chopped garlic and ginger.
5. Cook the mixture and add the tomatoes into it.
6. Add the spices.
7. When the tomatoes are done, add the quinoa into it.
8. Add in the broth.
9. Mix the ingredients carefully and cover your pan.
10. When your massaman is done, add in the cilantro.
11. Mix your massaman and let it cook for an additional five minutes.
12. Your dish is ready to be served.

3.4 Vegetarian Thai Pumpkin Curry Recipe

Preparation Time: 30 minutes

Cooking Time: 10 minutes

Serving: 4

Ingredients:

- Vegetable stock, two cups
- Minced garlic, one teaspoon
- Thai spices, two tablespoon
- Shallot, one
- Kaffir lime leaves, four
- Lime wedges
- Lemon grass, two sticks
- Fish sauce, two tablespoon
- Coconut milk, one cup
- Cilantro, a quarter cup
- Pumpkin pieces, half pound
- Olive oil, one tablespoon

Instructions:

1. Take a large sauce pan.
2. Add the shallots and olive oil.
3. Cook your shallots and then add the pumpkin pieces.
4. When the pumpkin pieces are half cooked, add the vegetable stock, and minced garlic.
5. Add the coconut milk and rest of the ingredients.
6. Cook your ingredients for ten minutes.
7. Garnish it with cilantro leaves.

8. Your dish is ready to be served.

3.5 Vegetarian Thai Baked Tofu with Noodles Recipe

Preparation Time: 10 minutes

Cooking Time: 20 minutes

Serving: 4

Ingredients:

- Powdered cumin, one tablespoon
- Salt, to taste
- Black pepper, to taste
- Turmeric powder, one teaspoon
- Onion, one cup
- Vegetable broth, one cup
- Smoked paprika, half teaspoon
- Dijon mustard, half cup
- Tofu pieces, one pound
- Minced garlic, two tablespoon
- Minced ginger, two tablespoon
- Cilantro, half cup
- Olive oil, two tablespoon
- Chopped tomatoes, one cup

- Cooked noodles, two cup

Instructions:

1. Take a pan.
2. Add in the oil and onions.
3. Cook the onions until they become soft and fragrant.
4. Add in the chopped garlic and ginger.
5. Cook the mixture and add the tomatoes into it.
6. Add the spices.
7. When the tomatoes are done, add the tofu pieces into it.
8. Mix the ingredients carefully.
9. Bake the tofu cubes for fifteen minutes.
10. When your tofu is done, mix it with the noodles.
11. Add in the cilantro.
12. Your dish is ready to be served.

3.6 Vegetarian Thai Curry Fettucini Recipe

Preparation Time: 30 minutes

Cooking Time: 10 minutes

Serving: 4

Ingredients:

- Water, two cups
- Rice noodles, one pack
- Galangal, one can
- Minced garlic, one teaspoon
- Minced ginger, one teaspoon
- Chopped onion, half cup
- Minced ginger, half tablespoon
- Lemon grass, two sticks
- Fish sauce, two tablespoon
- Coconut milk, one cup
- Cilantro, a quarter cup
- Olive oil, one tablespoon

Instructions:

1. Take a large sauce wok.
2. Add the chopped onion and olive oil.
3. Cook your chopped onion.
4. When the onions are cooked then add the galangal, minced garlic and ginger.
5. Add the coconut milk.
6. Cook your ingredients until they start boiling.
7. Add in the lemon grass and rest of the ingredients into your curry.
8. Now add the water and noodles into the dish.
9. Cook your ingredients for ten minutes.

10.   Garnish it with cilantro leaves.

11.   Your dish is ready to be served.

3.7 Vegetarian Thai Basil Fried Rice Recipe

Preparation Time: 30 minutes

Cooking Time: 10 minutes

Serving: 4

Ingredients:

- Thai fresh basil leaves, one cup
- Sliced green onions, half cup
- White peppercorns, one teaspoon
- Cilantro, one cup
- Fresh ginger, one teaspoon
- Fish sauce, one tablespoon
- Soy sauce, one tablespoon
- Chili garlic sauce, two tablespoon
- Fresh cilantro leaves, half cup
- Cooked rice, as required

Instructions:

1. Heat a large pan.

2. Add the vegetable broth and sauces into the mixture.

3. Cook your dish for ten minutes.

4. Add the cooked rice into the mixture.

5. Mix the rice well and cook it for five minutes.

6. Add the rest of the ingredients into the mixture.

7. Cook your dish for five more minutes.

8. Add the basil leaves and cilantro into the dish.

9. Mix your rice and then dish it out.

10. Your dish is ready to be served.

3.8 Vegetarian Thai Butternut Squash and Chickpea Curry Recipe

Preparation Time: 30 minutes

Cooking Time: 10 minutes

Serving: 4

Ingredients:

- Cooked chickpeas, two cup

- Vegetable stock, two cups
- Minced garlic, one teaspoon
- Thai spices, two tablespoon
- Shallot, one
- Kaffir lime leaves, four
- Lime wedges
- Lemon grass, two sticks
- Fish sauce, two tablespoon
- Coconut milk, one cup
- Cilantro, a quarter cup
- Butternut squash pieces, half pound
- Olive oil, one tablespoon

Instructions:

1. Take a large sauce pan.
2. Add the shallots and olive oil.
3. Cook your shallots and then add the butternut squash pieces.
4. When the butternut squash pieces are half cooked, add the galangal, vegetable stock, and minced garlic.
5. Add the cooked chickpeas into your curry.
6. Add the coconut milk and the rest of the ingredients.
7. Cook your ingredients for ten minutes.

8. Garnish it with cilantro leaves.

9. Your dish is ready to be served.

3.9 Vegetarian Thai Creamy Peanut Ramen Recipe

Preparation Time: 30 minutes

Cooking Time: 10 minutes

Serving: 4

Ingredients:

- Coconut cream, one cup
- Sliced green onions, half cup
- White peppercorns, one teaspoon
- Cilantro, one cup
- Fresh ginger, one teaspoon
- Fish sauce, one tablespoon
- Soy sauce, one tablespoon
- Chinese 5 spice, half teaspoon
- Chili garlic sauce, two tablespoon
- Fresh cilantro leaves, half cup
- Peanuts, two cups
- Minced lemon grass, one teaspoon
- Ramen, as required

Instructions:

12. Add all the ingredients of the sauce into a pan.

13. Add the coconut cream and the rest of the ingredients into the mixture.

14. Cook your dish for ten minutes.

15. Add the ramen into the mixture once the sauce is ready.

16. Mix the ramen well and cook it for five minutes.

17. Add the peanuts into the pan.

18. Cook your dish for five more minutes.

19. Add the cilantro into the dish.

20. Your dish is ready to be served.

3.10 Vegetarian Thai Chickpea and Sweet Potato Curry Recipe

Preparation Time: 30 minutes

Cooking Time: 10 minutes

Serving: 4

Ingredients
- Cooked chickpeas, two cup
- Vegetable stock, two cups
- Minced garlic, one teaspoon

- Thai spices, two tablespoon
- Shallot, one
- Kaffir lime leaves, four
- Lime wedges
- Lemon grass, two sticks
- Fish sauce, two tablespoon
- Coconut milk, one cup
- Cilantro, a quarter cup
- Sweet potato pieces, half pound
- Olive oil, one tablespoon

Instructions:
1. Take a large sauce pan.
2. Add the shallots and olive oil.
3. Cook your shallots and then add the sweet potato pieces.
4. When the sweet potato pieces are half cooked, add the galangal, vegetable stock, and minced garlic.
5. Add the cooked chickpeas into your curry.
6. Add the coconut milk and the rest of the ingredients.
7. Cook your ingredients for ten minutes.
8. Garnish it with cilantro leaves.
9. Your dish is ready to be served.

3.11 Vegetarian Thai Pineapple Rice Recipe

Preparation Time: 30 minutes

Cooking Time: 10 minutes

Serving: 4

Ingredients:

- Chopped pineapple pieces, one cup
- Sliced green onions, half cup
- White peppercorns, one teaspoon
- Cilantro, one cup
- Fresh ginger, one teaspoon
- Fish sauce, one tablespoon
- Soy sauce, one tablespoon
- Chili garlic sauce, two tablespoon
- Fresh cilantro leaves, half cup
- Cooked rice, as required

Instructions:

1. Heat a large pan.
2. Add the vegetable broth and sauces into the mixture.
3. Cook your dish for ten minutes.
4. Add the cooked rice into the mixture.
5. Mix the rice well and cook it for five minutes.
6. Add the rest of the ingredients into the mixture.
7. Cook your dish for five more minutes.
8. Add the chopped pineapple and cilantro into the dish.

9. Mix your rice and then dish it out.

10. Your dish is ready to be served.

3.12 Vegetarian Thai Tofu and Pepper Eggplant Recipe

Preparation Time: 30 minutes

Cooking Time: 10 minutes

Serving: 4

Ingredients:

- Eggplant cubes, two cups
- Red bell pepper, one cup
- Yellow bell pepper, one cup
- Green bell pepper, one cup
- Sliced green onions, half cup
- White peppercorns, one teaspoon

- Cilantro, one cup
- Fresh ginger, one teaspoon
- Fish sauce, one tablespoon
- Soy sauce, one tablespoon
- Chili paste, one tablespoon
- Tofu cubes, two cup
- Chili garlic sauce, two tablespoon
- Fresh cilantro leaves, half cup
- Fresh basil leaves, a quarter cup
- Vegetable broth, one cup

Instructions:

1. Add all the ingredients of the sauce into a wok.
2. Add the chili paste, eggplant, bell peppers, vegetable broth and sauces into the mixture.
3. Cook your dish for ten minutes.
4. Add the tofu cubes and the rest of the ingredients into the mixture once the sauce is ready.
5. Mix the tofu cubes well and cook them for five minutes.
6. Add the cilantro into the dish.
7. Your dish is ready to be served.

3.13 Vegetarian Thai Baby Corn and Vegetables Stir-Fry Recipe

Preparation Time: 10 minutes

Cooking Time: 20 minutes

Serving: 4

Ingredients:

- Fish sauce, two tablespoon
- Soy sauce, half cup
- Tomatoes, two
- Baby corn, two cups
- Cilantro, half cup
- Salt and pepper, to taste
- Minced ginger, half tablespoon
- Vegetable oil, two tablespoon
- Red chili peppers, three
- Onion, one
- Mixed vegetables, one cup
- Scallions, half cup
- Minced garlic, one teaspoon

Instructions:

1. In a large wok, add the shallots and oil.
2. Cook the shallots and then add the ginger and garlic.
3. Cook the ginger and garlic.

4. Add the mixed vegetables, baby corn and the rest of the ingredients into your dish except the toasted nuts.

5. Cook your dish for five minutes.

6. Garnish your dish with cilantro.

7. Your dish is ready to be served.

3.14 Vegetarian Thai Tofu and Coconut Curry Recipe

Preparation Time: 30 minutes

Cooking Time: 10 minutes

Serving: 4

Ingredients:

- Unsweetened shredded coconut, one cup
- Vegetable stock, two cups
- Minced garlic, one teaspoon
- Thai spices, two tablespoon
- Shallot, one
- Galangal, half teaspoon

- Mixed vegetables, half cup
- Kaffir lime leaves, four
- Lemon grass, two sticks
- Fish sauce, two tablespoon
- Coconut milk, one cup
- Cilantro, a quarter cup
- Tofu cubes, half pound
- Olive oil, one tablespoon

Instructions:

1. Take a large sauce pan.
2. Add the shallots and olive oil.
3. Cook your shallots and then add the vegetables and tofu cubes.
4. Add the galangal, vegetable stock, and minced garlic.
5. Add the coconut milk.
6. Add the unsweetened shredded coconut and the rest of the ingredients.
7. Cook your ingredients for ten minutes.
8. Garnish it with cilantro leaves.
9. Your dish is ready to be served.

3.15 Vegetarian Thai Lentils in Peanut Sauce Recipe

Preparation Time: 30 minutes

Cooking Time: 10 minutes

Serving: 4

Ingredients:
- Mixed lentils, two cups
- Minced garlic, one teaspoon
- Minced ginger, one teaspoon
- Chopped onion, half cup
- Minced ginger, half tablespoon
- Lemon grass, two sticks
- Fish sauce, two tablespoon
- Spicy peanut sauce, one cup
- Coconut milk, one cup
- Cilantro, a quarter cup
- Olive oil, one tablespoon

Instructions:
10. Take a large sauce pan.
11. Add the chopped onion and olive oil.
12. Cook your chopped onion and then add the lentils.
13. Add the coconut milk.

14. Cook your ingredients until they start boiling.

15. Add in the spicy peanut sauce and the rest of the ingredients.

16. Cook your ingredients for ten minutes.

17. Garnish it with cilantro leaves.

18. Your dish is ready to be served.

3.16 Vegetarian Thai Black Pepper and Garlic Tofu Recipe

Preparation Time: 30 minutes

Cooking Time: 20 minutes

Serving: 4

Ingredients:
- Minced garlic, two tablespoon
- Minced ginger, two tablespoon
- Cilantro, half cup
- Olive oil, two tablespoon
- Chopped tomatoes, one cup
- Powdered cumin, one tablespoon
- Salt, to taste
- Black pepper, two tablespoon
- Turmeric powder, one teaspoon
- Onion, one cup
- Vegetable broth, one cup

- Smoked paprika, half teaspoon
- Water, half cup
- Tofu cubes, one pound

Instructions:

1. Take a wok.
2. Add in the oil and onions.
3. Cook the onions until they become soft and fragrant.
4. Add in the chopped garlic and ginger.
5. Cook the mixture and add the tomatoes into it.
6. Add the spices.
7. When the tomatoes are done, add the tofu cubes into it.
8. Mix the tofu so that the tomatoes and spices are coated all over the tofu.
9. Cook for five minutes.
10. Add in the water.
11. Mix the ingredients carefully and cover your wok.
12. When your tofu is done, add in the cilantro.
13. Your dish is ready to be served.

3.17 Vegetarian Thai Panang Curry with Vegetables Recipe

Preparation Time: 30 minutes

Cooking Time: 10 minutes

Serving: 4

Ingredients:

- Panang curry paste, two tablespoon
- Vegetable stock, two cups
- Minced garlic, one teaspoon
- Thai spices, two tablespoon
- Shallot, one
- Galangal, half teaspoon
- Kaffir lime leaves, four
- Lemon grass, two sticks
- Fish sauce, two tablespoon
- Coconut milk, one cup
- Cilantro, a quarter cup
- Mixed vegetables, half pound
- Olive oil, one tablespoon

Instructions:

1. Take a large sauce pan.
2. Add the shallots and olive oil.
3. Cook your shallots and then add the mixed vegetables.
4. Add the galangal, vegetable stock, and minced garlic.

5. Add the coconut milk and pananag curry paste.

6. Add the rest of the ingredients.

7. Cook your ingredients for ten minutes.

8. Garnish it with cilantro leaves.

9. Your dish is ready to be served.

3.18 Vegetarian Thai Tofu in Peanut Butter Sauce Recipe

Preparation Time: 30 minutes

Cooking Time: 10 minutes

Serving: 4

Ingredients:
- Tofu cubes, two cups
- Minced garlic, one teaspoon
- Minced ginger, one teaspoon
- Chopped onion, half cup
- Minced ginger, half tablespoon
- Lemon grass, two sticks

- Fish sauce, two tablespoon
- Peanut butter sauce, one cup
- Coconut milk, one cup
- Cilantro, a quarter cup
- Olive oil, one tablespoon

Instructions:

1. Take a large sauce pan.
2. Add the chopped onion and olive oil.
3. Cook your chopped onion and then add the tofu.
4. Add the coconut milk.
5. Cook your ingredients until they start boiling.
6. Add in the peanut butter sauce and the rest of the ingredients.
7. Cook your ingredients for ten minutes.
8. Garnish it with cilantro leaves.
9. Your dish is ready to be served.

Chapter 4: The World of Vegetarian Thai Dessert

This chapter focuses on healthy Thai vegetarian dessert recipes that you will find very easy to make on your own.

4.1 Vegetarian Thai Caramelized Coconut Cake Recipe

Preparation Time: 10 minutes

Cooking Time: 20 minutes

Serving: 4

Ingredients:

- Coconut milk, one cup
- Coconut flakes, half cup
- Baking powder, four teaspoon
- Eggs, two
- Whole wheat flour, half cup
- Baking soda, one teaspoon
- Rice flour, one cup
- Sugar, half cup
- Vanilla extract, one tablespoon

Instructions:

1. In a large bowl, add the eggs.
2. Beat the eggs until they turn creamy and frothy.
3. Add the melted butter and coconut milk into the mixture.
4. Add the sugar and beat the mixture for five more minutes.
5. In a separate bowl, add all the dried ingredients.
6. Slowly add your dried mixture into your wet mixture.
7. Add the vanilla extract as required.
8. Bake your cake for ten to fifteen minutes.
9. When done, dish it out on a rack.
10. Your dish is ready to be served.

4.2 Vegetarian Thai Mango Dessert Recipe

Preparation Time: 10 minutes

Cooking Time: 20 minutes

Serving: 4

Ingredients:

- Sliced mangoes, one cup
- Rice, one cup
- Baking powder, four teaspoon

- Coconut milk, one cup
- All-purpose flour, one and a half cup
- Baking soda, one teaspoon
- Eggs, two
- Brown sugar, one cup
- Tapioca starch, one tablespoon
- Salt, to taste

Instructions:

1. In a large bowl, add the eggs.
2. Beat the eggs until they turn frothy.
3. Add the baking powder and coconut milk into it.
4. Add the brown sugar and beat the mixture for five more minutes.
5. In a separate bowl, add all the dried ingredients.
6. Mix them thoroughly.
7. Cook the rice in rice cooking pan.
8. Add the salt and pepper as required.
9. Put the mango slices on cooked rice.
10. Your dish is ready to be served.

4.3 Vegetarian Thai Mung Bean Pudding Recipe

Preparation Time: 10 minutes

Cooking Time: 20 minutes

Serving: 4

Ingredients:

- Mung beans, one cup
- Baking powder, four teaspoon
- Barley flakes, one and a half cup
- Baking soda, one teaspoon
- Buttermilk, two cups
- White sugar, one cup
- Water, two cups
- Tapioca flour, one cup
- Coconut cream, half cup

Instructions:

1. In a large bowl, add the tapioca flour into it.
2. Add the mung beans into the mixture.
3. Add the white sugar and beat the mixture for five more minutes.
4. In a separate bowl, add all the dried ingredients.
5. Add the water into it
6. Add the coconut cream into the mixture.
7. Mix them thoroughly until a homogeneous mixture is obtained.
8. Check the thickness of pudding and add sugar and flour if required.
9. Your dish is ready to be served.

4.4 Vegetarian Thai Coconut Black Rice Pudding Recipe

Preparation Time: 20 minutes

Cooking Time: 20 minutes

Serving: 4

Ingredients:

- Cooked black rice, one bowl
- Cilantro, as required
- Baking powder, four teaspoon
- Coconut flakes, one and a half cup
- Baking soda, one teaspoon
- Buttermilk, two cups
- White sugar, one cup
- Water, two cups
- Tapioca flour, one cup
- Coconut cream, half cup

Instructions:

1. In a large bowl, add the tapioca flour into it.
2. Add the white sugar into the mixture as required.

3. Add the baking powder and beat the mixture for five more minutes.

4. In a separate bowl, add the water in it.

5. Add coconut flakes into it.

6. Add the coconut cream into the mixture.

7. Add the cooked rice into it.

8. Mix them thoroughly until a consistent mixture is formed.

9. Check the thickness of pudding and add sugar and flour if required.

10.   Your dish is ready to be served.

4.5 Vegetarian Thai Sticky Banana Rice Recipe

Preparation Time: 10 minutes

Cooking Time: 20 minutes

Serving: 4

Ingredients:

- Sweet rice, two cup
- Banana leaves, five
- Bananas, five
- Salt, a pinch
- Bread flour, half cup
- Coconut milk, one cup
- Lime zest, as required

- Pepper, to taste
- Soy sauce, one tablespoon

Instructions:

1. In a large bowl, add the bread flour into it.
2. Cook the rice in the rice cooking pan.
3. Add the rice into it and mix them.
4. Add the lime zest as required.
5. Add the cilantro if required.
6. Add the banana leaves into the mixture.
7. Add the banana pieces into it.
8. Add some water and boil the whole mixture for ten minutes.
9. Your dish is ready to be served.

4.6 Thai Bananas in Coconut Milk Recipe

Preparation Time: 10 minutes

Cooking Time: 20 minutes

Serving: 4

Ingredients:

- Coconut milk, one cup
- Bananas, five
- Salt, a pinch
- Bread flour, half cup
- Coconut milk, one cup
- Lime zest, as required
- Pepper, to taste
- Brown sugar, two tablespoon

Instructions:

1. Heat a large pan.
2. Take a bowl and add the coconut milk into it.
3. Add the banana pieces into it.
4. Add the lime zest as required.
5. Add the cilantro and rest of the ingredients if required.
6. Add the mixture into the pan.
7. Add some water and simmer the whole mixture for ten minutes.
8. Your dish is ready to be served.

4.7 Thai Mung Bean Sweets Recipe

Preparation Time: 10 minutes

Cooking Time: 20 minutes

Serving: 4

Ingredients:

- Mung beans, one cup
- Baking powder, four teaspoon
- Barley flakes, one and a half cup
- Baking soda, one teaspoon
- Buttermilk, two cups
- White sugar, one cup
- Water, two cups
- Tapioca flour, one cup
- Coconut cream, half cup

Instructions:

1. In a large bowl, add the tapioca flour into it.
2. Add the mung beans into the mixture.
3. Add the white sugar and beat the mixture for five more minutes.
4. In a separate bowl, add all the dried ingredients.
5. Add the water into it.
6. Add the coconut cream into the mixture.
7. Mix them thoroughly until a consistent mixture is formed.
8. Cook your mixture until it thickens.
9. Switch off the stove.

10.   Make small round structures from the mixture.

11.   Your dish is ready to be served.

4.8 Thai Mango and Coconut Sauce Recipe

Preparation Time: 10 minutes

Cooking Time: 20 minutes

Serving: 4

Ingredients:
- Sliced mangoes, one cup
- Coconut milk, one cup
- Lime zest, as required
- Red bell pepper, one tablespoon
- Pepper, to taste
- Salt, to taste

Instructions:
1. Take a bowl and add the coconut milk into it.
2. Add the lime zest into it.
3. Add the salt and pepper as required.
4. Add the cilantro if required.
5. In the end, add the Mango slices into the mixture.
6. Boil the whole mixture for ten minutes
7. Your dish is ready to be served.

4.9 Thai Rice Balls in Coconut Milk Recipe

Preparation Time: 10 minutes

Cooking Time: 20 minutes

Serving: 4

Ingredients:

- Coconut milk, one cup
- Rice balls, one cup
- Salt, a pinch
- Bread flour, half cup
- Coconut milk, one cup
- Lime zest, as required
- Pepper, to taste
- Brown sugar, two tablespoon

Instructions:

1. Heat a large pan.
2. Take a bowl and add the coconut milk into it.
3. Add the rice balls into it.
4. Add the lime zest as required.
5. Add the cilantro and rest of the ingredients if required.
6. Add the mixture into the pan.

7. Add some water and simmer the whole mixture for ten minutes.

8. Your dish is ready to be served.

4.10 Thai Coconut Balls Recipe

Preparation Time: 10 minutes

Cooking Time: 10 minutes

Serving: 4

Ingredients:

- Glutinous rice flour, three cups
- Sweetened shredded coconut, a quarter cup
- Vegetable oil, two tablespoon
- Brown sugar, two cups
- Coconut milk, a quarter cup
- Sweetened red bean paste, one cup

Instructions:

1. Heat a wok.
2. Add the vegetable oil in the wok.
3. Add the sweetened shredded coconut.
4. Cook them for five minutes.
5. Add the glutinous rice flour and brown sugar into the wok.
6. Add the coconut milk and sweetened red bean paste into the mixture.

7. Cook your dish and then dish it out.

8. When the mixture turns a little cold, make small round balls from the mixture.

9. Your dish is ready to be served.

4.11 Thai Style Crème Caramel Recipe

Preparation Time: 10 minutes

Cooking Time: 30 minutes

Serving: 6

Ingredients:
- Palm sugar, half cup
- Eggs, four
- Caster sugar, two cups
- Vanilla essence, one teaspoon
- Coconut milk, one cup

Instructions:
1. Take a large bowl.
2. Add the eggs into the bowl.
3. Beat the eggs well.
4. When they turn fluffy, add the palm sugar into it and beat the mixture well.
5. Make sure your sugar dissolves into the mixture.
6. Add the vanilla essence and coconut milk into the mixture.

7. Add the mixture in non-stick mold.

8. Bake your mixture for ten minutes.

9. Dish out and sprinkle the caster sugar on top.

10. Your dish is ready to be served.

4.12 Thai Fried Banana Rolls Recipe

Preparation Time: 10 minutes

Cooking Time: 10 minutes

Serving: 2

Ingredients:
- Chopped bananas, five
- Shredded coconut, half cup
- Wonton wraps, as required
- Chinese five spice, as needed
- Cooking oil, as required

Instructions:
7. In a large bowl, mix all the ingredients together.

8. Add the mixture into the wonton wrappers.

9. Wrap your rolls.

10. Fry your rolls until they turn golden brown.

11. Dish out and drizzle any sauce if you want on top.

12. Your dish is ready to be served.

4.13 Thai Sticky Rice Cake Recipe

Preparation Time: 10 minutes

Cooking Time: 20 minutes

Serving: 4

Ingredients:

- Sweet rice, two cups
- Banana leaves, five
- Bananas, five
- Salt, a pinch
- Bread flour, half cup
- Coconut milk, one cup
- Lime zest, as required
- Pepper, to taste
- Baking powder, one teaspoon
- Vanilla essence, half teaspoon
- Soy sauce, one tablespoon

Instructions:

1. In a large bowl, add the bread flour into it.
2. Cook the rice in the rice cooking pan.
3. Add the rice into it and mix them.
4. Add the lime zest as required.

5. Add the cilantro if required.

6. Add the banana leaves into the mixture.

7. Add the banana pieces into it.

8. Add some water and boil the whole mixture for ten minutes.

9. Cool your mixture and then add the vanilla essence, baking powder and coconut milk into it.

10.   Mix your ingredients.

11.   Bake your rice cake.

12.   When your cake is done, dish it out and slice it up.

13.   Your dish is ready to be served.

4.14 Thai Mangosteen Custard Recipe

Preparation Time: 30 minutes

Cooking Time: 10 minutes

Serving: 4

Ingredients:

- Mangosteen cubes, one cup

- Eggs, two
- Coconut, two
- Chinese sweet spices, to taste
- Coconut milk, half cup
- White sugar, half cup
- Salt, one teaspoon
- Lemon extract, one teaspoon
- Almond extract, one teaspoon
- All-purpose flour, two cups
- Butter, one cup

Instructions:

13. Take a medium bowl and add the eggs and the tapioca flour in it.

14. Add one cup of coconut milk and mix well.

15. Add the sugar, salt and the beaten eggs.

16. Mix them well.

17. Mix the warm milk mixture with the flour and the coconut.

18. Add the eggs, lemon extract and almond extract together.

19. Add the baking soda in the mixture.

20. Simmer it for few minutes.

21. Add the mangosteen cubes in the end.

22. Check the thickness of the custard.

23. Your dish is ready to be served.

4.15 Thai Mango Layered Custard Recipe

Preparation Time: 30 minutes

Cooking Time: 10 minutes

Serving: 4

Ingredients:

- Mango cubes, one cup
- Eggs, two
- Coconut, two
- Chinese sweet spices, to taste
- Coconut milk, half cup
- White sugar, half cup
- Salt, one teaspoon
- Lemon extract, one teaspoon
- Almond extract, one teaspoon
- All-purpose flour, two cups
- Butter, one cup

Instructions:

1. Take a medium bowl and add the eggs and the tapioca flour in it.
2. Add the one cup coconut milk and mix well.
3. Add the sugar, salt and the beaten eggs.

4. Mix them well.

5. Mix the warm milk mixture with the flour and the coconut.

6. Add the eggs, lemon extract and almond extract together.

7. Add the baking soda in the mixture.

8. Simmer it for a few minutes.

9. Check the thickness of the custard.

10. In a large bowl, spread some of the custard mixture in the end.

11. Add a layer of the mongo cubes.

12. Add a layer of the custard again.

13. Complete your layered custard.

14. Your dish is ready to be served.

Chapter 5: The World of Vegetarian Thai Snack Recipes

Following are some classic vegetarian Thai snack recipes that are rich in healthy nutrients and you can easily make them with the detailed instructions list in each recipe:

5.1 Vegetarian Thai Peanut Cauliflower Wings Recipe

Preparation Time: 10 minutes

Cooking Time: 20 minutes

Serving: 4

Ingredients:

- Cauliflower florets, one cup
- Flour, one cup
- Almond milk, one cup
- Garlic powder, one tablespoon
- Peanut butter, one cup
- Soy sauce, one tablespoon
- Sesame oil, one tablespoon
- Lime juice, one tablespoon
- Coconut sugar, two teaspoon

- Ginger, one tablespoon
- Water, two cups
- Sesame seeds, for topping
- Green onion, for topping

Instructions:

1. Take a bowl and add the flour in it.
2. Add the almond milk and garlic powder.
3. Mix them thoroughly.
4. Then add salt and pepper as required.
5. Take a baking pan and add the cauliflower florets into it.
6. Bake it for twenty minutes.
7. Mix the sauce ingredients in a bowl.
8. Mix the sauce and cauliflower in a bowl together.
9. Use sesame seeds and the green onions for topping.
10. Your dish is ready to be served.

5.2 Vegetarian Thai Cabbage Salad Recipe

Preparation Time: 10 minutes

Cooking Time: 25 minutes

Serving: 4

Ingredients:

- Sesame seeds, as required
- Shredded red cabbage, two cups
- Carrot sliced, one cup
- Red bell pepper sliced, one cup
- Chopped mango, half cup
- Green onion, half cup
- Coriander leaves, half cup
- Thai red chili, half cup
- Peanut butter, two tablespoon
- Lime juice, one tablespoon
- Ginger, one tablespoon
- Garlic powder, two teaspoon
- Maple syrup, half teaspoon
- Sesame oil, one teaspoon
- Soy sauce, one teaspoon
- Sriracha, one tablespoon
- Salt, to taste
- Pepper, to taste

Instructions:

1. Take a large bowl and add all the vegetables one by one
2. Add the ginger and garlic powder.
3. Mix well.
4. Add the peanuts and mix gently
5. Add lime juice, maple syrup, Thai red chili and soy sauce.
6. Add the salt and pepper as you like.
7. Add the sesame oil and sesame seeds and mix well.
8. Add the sriracha into the mixture.
9. Mix all ingredients and make good combination.
10. Your salad is ready to be served.

5.3 Vegetarian Thai Slow with Ginger Peanut Dressing Recipe

Preparation Time: 30 minutes

Cooking Time: 25 minutes

Serving: 4

Ingredients:
- Ginger, two tablespoon
- Peanuts, one cup
- Carrot sliced, one cup
- Red bell pepper sliced, one cup

- Green onion, half cup
- Coriander leaves, half cup
- Thai red chili, half cup
- Peanut butter, two tablespoon
- Lime juice, one tablespoon
- Ginger, one tablespoon
- Garlic powder, two teaspoon
- Maple syrup, half teaspoon
- Sesame oil, one teaspoon
- Salt, to taste
- Pepper, to taste

Instructions:

1. Take a large bowl and add all the vegetables one by one.
2. Add the ginger and garlic powder.
3. Mix well until a good mixture is obtained.
4. Add the peanuts and mix gently.
5. Add lime juice, maple syrup, Thai red chili and soy sauce.
6. Add the salt and pepper as you like.
7. Add the maple syrup, red bell peppers and peanut butter.
8. Add the sriracha into the mixture.
9. Mix all ingredients and pour the ginger and the peanuts on top.
10. Your salad is ready to be served.

5.4 Vegetarian Thai Chickpea Salad with Curry Peanut Dressing Recipe

Preparation Time: 20 minutes

Cooking Time: 20 minutes

Serving: 4

Ingredients:
- Chickpea, one bowl
- Curry Peanuts, one cup
- Carrot sliced, one cup
- Red bell pepper sliced, one cup
- Green onion, half cup
- Coriander leaves, half cup
- Thai red chili, half cup
- Peanut butter, two tablespoon
- Lime juice, one tablespoon
- Ginger, one tablespoon
- Garlic powder, two teaspoon
- Maple syrup, half teaspoon
- Sesame oil, one teaspoon
- Salt, to taste
- Pepper, to taste

Instructions:

1. Take a large bowl and add all the vegetables one by one.

2. Add the ginger and garlic powder to it.

3. Mix well until a good mixture is obtained.

4. Add the peanuts and mix gently

5. Add lime juice, maple syrup, Thai red chili and soy sauce.

6. Add the salt and pepper as you like.

7. Add the maple syrup, red bell peppers and peanut butter.

8. Add the sriracha into the mixture.

9. Mix all ingredients and pour the chickpea and curry peanut on the top.

10. Your salad is ready to be served.

5.5 Vegetarian Thai Kale and Cabbage Salad Recipe

Preparation Time: 20 minutes

Cooking Time: 20 minutes

Serving: 2

Ingredients:

- Cabbage, one cup
- Thai kale, one cup
- Carrot sliced, one cup
- Red bell pepper sliced, one cup
- Green onion, half cup

- Coriander leaves, half cup
- Thai red chili, half cup
- Peanut butter, two tablespoon
- Lime juice, one tablespoon
- Ginger, one tablespoon
- Garlic powder, two teaspoon
- Maple syrup, half teaspoon
- Sesame oil, one teaspoon
- Salt, to taste
- Pepper, to taste

Instructions:

1. Take a large bowl and add all the vegetables one by one.
2. Add the ginger and garlic powder to it.
3. Mix well until a good mixture is formed.
4. Add the peanuts and mix gently.
5. Add lime juice, maple syrup, Thai red chili and soy sauce.
6. Add the salt and pepper as you like.
7. Add the maple syrup, red bell peppers and peanut butter.
8. Add the sriracha into the mixture.
9. Add the kale slices and cabbage into the mixture.
10. Your salad is ready to be served.

5.6 Vegetarian Thai Peanuts and Noodles Salad Recipe

Preparation Time: 10 minutes

Cooking Time: 20 minutes

Serving: 4

Ingredients:
- Peanuts, one cup
- Noodles, one pack
- Carrot sliced, one cup
- Red bell pepper sliced, one cup
- Green onion, half cup
- Coriander leaves, half cup
- Thai red chili, half cup
- Peanut butter, two tablespoon
- Lime juice, one tablespoon
- Ginger, one tablespoon
- Garlic powder, two teaspoon
- Maple syrup, half teaspoon
- Sesame oil, one teaspoon
- Salt, to taste
- Pepper, to taste

Instructions:

1. Take a large bowl and add the boiling water into it.
2. Prepare noodles in it for five minutes.
3. Add the ginger and garlic powder to it.
4. Mix well until a good mixture is obtained.
5. Add the peanuts and mix gently.
6. Add lime juice, maple syrup, Thai red chili and soy sauce.
7. Add the salt and pepper as you like.
8. Add the maple syrup, red bell peppers and peanut butter.
9. Add the noodles into the mixture.
10. Your salad is ready to be served.

5.7 Vegetarian Thai Satay Rolls Recipe

Preparation Time: 30 minutes

Cooking Time: 25 minutes

Serving: 4

Ingredients:

- Baby arugula, one cup
- Cilantro, one
- Red bell pepper, one tablespoon
- Cucumber, two

- Peanut butter, half cup
- Coconut milk, one cup
- Garlic powder, two tablespoon
- Ginger, one tablespoon
- Soy sauce, one tablespoon
- Lime juice, one tablespoon
- Brown sugar, two tablespoon

Instructions:

1. Heat the water in a pan.
2. Dip the rice paper into the warm water.
3. Add the cilantro, mint, bell pepper and cucumbers into it.
4. Add the peanut butter, coconut milk into it.
5. Add the ginger and the garlic powder as required.
6. Add the brown sugar as required.
7. Season it with the salt and pepper.
8. Tightly roll the rice paper over all the ingredients.
9. Serve the rolls with soy sauce.

5.8 Vegetarian Thai Corn and Zucchini Fritters Recipe

Preparation Time: 30 minutes

Cooking Time: 5 minutes

Serving: 4

Ingredients:

- All-purpose flour, one cup
- Fresh corn, half cup
- Baking powder, one cup
- Cumin, half tablespoon
- Salt, one tablespoon
- Milk, one cup
- Black pepper, one tablespoon
- Eggs, two
- Butter, half cup
- Oil, one cup

Instructions:

1. Take a large bowl and add the flour into it.
2. Add the sugar, salt, the pepper and cumin.
3. Mix them well.
4. Take another bowl and add the eggs and milk into it.
5. Add the butter and mix the ingredients.

6. Stir it in the zucchini, corn and cheese.

7. Mix them thoroughly.

8. Warm the oil in the skillet.

9. Fry the mixture until it becomes brown and crispy.

10. Your dish is ready to be served.

5.9 Vegetarian Thai Curry Tacos Recipe

Preparation Time: 30 minutes

Cooking Time: 10 minutes

Serving: 4

Ingredients:

- Thai red curry paste, two tablespoon
- Canola oil, one cup
- Minced garlic, two tablespoon
- Chopped red onion, one cup
- Coconut milk, one cup
- Lime juice, two tablespoon
- Water, as required
- Cilantro leaves, as required
- Salt, a pinch
- Taco shells, as required
- Avocado sliced, two

Instructions:

1. Add the canola oil into the skillet.
2. Add the curry paste and garlic powder.
3. Cook it for five minutes.
4. Add more oil into it and add all the ingredients.
5. Add the salt and pepper as required.
6. Cook it for few minutes more.
7. Add the ingredients into the taco shells.
8. Your dish is ready to be served.

5.10 Spicy Vegetarian Thai Grapefruit Salad Recipe

Preparation Time: 30 minutes

Cooking Time: 50 minutes

Serving: 5

Ingredients:

- Grape fruits, one cup
- Tomatoes, one or two
- Carrot sliced, one cup
- Red bell pepper sliced, one cup
- Green onion, half cup
- Coriander leaves, half cup

- Thai red chili, half cup
- Peanut butter, two tablespoon
- Lime juice, one tablespoon
- Ginger, one tablespoon
- Garlic powder, two teaspoon
- Maple syrup, half teaspoon
- Sesame oil, one teaspoon
- Salt, to taste
- Pepper, to taste

Instructions:

1. Take a large bowl and add the peeled grapefruit and the vegetables one by one.
2. Add the ginger and garlic powder to it.
3. Mix well until a good mixture is formed.
4. Add the peanuts and mix gently
5. Add lime juice, maple syrup, Thai red chili and soy sauce.
6. Add the salt and pepper as you like.
7. Add the maple syrup, red bell peppers and peanut butter.
8. Add the sriracha into the mixture.
9. Mix all ingredients well so that a homogeneous mixture is obtained.
10. Your salad is ready to be served.

Conclusion

Thailand is the most acclaimed nation in the whole world for its cooking. Traversing from the southern landmass toward the northern regions, the nation offers a various mix of madly flavorful food. Thai food is not the only cuisine to have been changed in the excursion across seas. Various vegetarian Thai foods are loved across the world and you in particular would enjoy cooking your vegetarian food with the Thai flavors inserted in them.

The different flavours utilized in Thai cooking have tremendous measure of astounding properties that soundly affects our general wellbeing. This cookbook incorporates 70 healthy plans that contain vegetarian breakfast, vegetarian lunch, vegetarian dinner, vegetarian dessert and vegetarian snack recipes that you can undoubtedly make at home without the help of any kind. Anyway, why order or go out for Thai food when you can be the culinary Thai expert at your home? Start reading and start cooking with this amazing and easy cookbook.

CPSIA information can be obtained
at www.ICGtesting.com
Printed in the USA
LVHW011204290721
693967LV00012B/917